~~79~~ 80 Things *you* MUST DO to be a GREAT BOSS

08

6 l

~~79~~ 80 THINGS YOU MUST DO TO BE A GREAT BOSS

How to focus on the fundamentals of managing people properly

David Freemantle

The McGraw-Hill Companies

London · New York · St Louis · San Francisco · Auckland
Bogotá · Caracas · Lisbon · Madrid · Mexico
Milan · Montreal · New Delhi · Panama · Paris · San Juan
São Paulo · Singapore · Sydney · Tokyo · Toronto

Published by
McGraw-Hill Publishing Company
Shoppenhangers Road, Maidenhead, Berkshire SL6 2QL, England
Telephone 01628 23432
Fax 01628 770224

British Library Cataloguing in Publication Data

Freemantle, David
    80 Things You Must Do to be a Great Boss:
    How to Focus on the Fundamentals of Managing People Properly
    I. Title
    658.3

    ISBN 0-07-709043-8

Library of Congress Cataloging-in-Publication Data

Freemantle, David.
    80 things you must do to be a great boss: how to focus on the
    fundamentals of managing properly / David Freemantle.
        p.   cm.
    ISBN 0-07-709043-8
    1. Management.   2. Executive ability.   I. Title.   II. Title:
Eighty things you must do to be a great boss.
HD31.F753
658.4–dc20   94-45693
                                                                  CIP

Reprinted 1997

McGraw-Hill

A Division of The McGraw-Hill Companies

Typeset by BookEns Limited, Royston, Herts.
and printed and bound in Great Britain at the University Press, Cambridge

Printed on permanent paper in compliance with ISO Standard 9706

Contents

The ~~79~~ 80 things

Contents

Introduction

(NB: The term 'management' is used in this book to refer specifically to the 'management of people' as opposed to other non-people management tasks, such as financial management or property management.)

There is an illusion of progress in many organizations. This illusion covers modern management practice. It is portrayed (if not betrayed) by the replacement of last year's centralized initiative with some new crusade to reform the organization. As ever, the cynics will tell you, 'We've seen it all before, this fad will die the same death as all the others'. The new crusade inevitably will attempt to solve the organization's intractable problems using some miracle cure advocated by external hyped-up evangelists and sold to wide-eyed managers who soon become the organization's own internal hyped-up evangelists.

The cure, of course, is based on some seductive new theory of management. The senior bosses will like it because the cure enables them to go on managing in their bad old ways while some inconsequential person is assigned the task of resolving the organization's problems by putting into practice this latest curative technique. Few will admit, at least openly, that these problems are of the senior bosses' making. It is always somebody else, it is always 'them' who are causing the problems with quality, or performance, or morale, or communications. The stool-pigeon who has been assigned the task is invariably a 'convert to the cause' and will go about with evangelical zeal setting up working parties and training courses to implement Total Quality Management, or performance appraisal, or empowerment, or Management By Objectives or whatever the crusading cause is.

There is no miracle cure for management problems. In fact, there is no new theory of modern management. There never will be and there never has been. Talking about modern management practice is like talking about modern marriage. Modern marriage is resulting in more and more divorces, despite the lure of sex education videos, new counselling techniques, and other attempts at marital therapy.

Success in management, like success in marriage, is all about getting some fundamental basics right – basics that get obscured by new techniques peddled by experts for 'do-gooding' reasons or for financial gain.

This book is all about those basics of people management and the things any good boss should do to return to them.

To be honest, most managers and their people are fed up to their back teeth with the latest initiative from the centre, telling them how to do their job. These initiatives are often from self-righteous, inexperienced, empire-building centralists who delude themselves into thinking that they know best. They attempt thought reform, attitudinal change, or behaviour improvement with the use of whizzy techniques. There are reminiscences of Chairman Mao as the edict is issued: 'You must think *quality*' (as if we have never thought *quality* before, as if we have never done anything about quality in our lives, as if the thought of implementing total quality was an amazing gem of wisdom from our esteemed chairman who is fighting a heroic battle against the enemies of the organization who seek to destroy it with substandard production). The drums are banged, the 'think quality' posters are put up, and hordes of red guards are mobilized through expensive thought-reform programmes of education, 'You must think like the Chairman, *quality* is all important'.

Dissenters are branded as cynics, troublemakers and 'the negative element'. They are assigned to the gulag outreaches of the organization, never to be promoted, and stripped bare of the 'merit increase' and bonus privileges enjoyed by the deferential and loyal masses so beloved of the Chairman.

One manager, frustrated by his inability to do his real job, described the syndrome as 'initiative fatigue'. His seniors were forever hijacking his time to sit on working parties, steering groups and other committees to pursue one or more of the latest fads (initiatives) being pursued by his employer. Invariably these initiatives achieved nothing and frequently much less. Thought reform never occurred, nor did quality or performance ever improve.

You only have to make a cursory study of the more successful business leaders of our time to realize that most of them do not practise what the management theorists advocate they should. These leaders, while frequently entertained by the evangelists are rarely attracted to their theories and even more rarely put them into practice. There seems to be a huge, yawning gap between what is taught by the evangelists (and subsequently the textbook academics) on how to manage people and the actual practices pursued by many successful business people.

That gap is common sense. Common sense does not lend itself to theory, nor to evangelism, nor to lengthy training courses, yet the more successful managers are merchants of common-sense thinking and common-sense practice. In pursuing the latest theory, too many managers leave their senses behind them to divorce themselves from the very people they should be relating to more closely.

To manage people properly you do not have to rely on, or even use, the complicated and bureaucratic techniques peddled by academics and evangelical consultants. All you need is a healthy dose of common sense – and, in case it eludes you – the ability to question yourself on what is, in fact, common sense. Without that ability to challenge yourself, common sense often becomes distorted sense. The more difficult task is to put common sense into practice. It is common sense not to smoke, not to overeat and not to consume too much alcohol. That much is known. The difficult task is to stop smoking, to slim, to reduce alcohol intake. Common sense dictates that the solution is provided by applying mind over matter – no gimmicky technique can substitute for that. It is well proven that pursuing the latest dietary fad does not result in long-term weight loss.

The same applies to managing people. It is all about the mind of the boss and what matters to him or her. The definition of 'what matters' can be found through common sense and a simple interpretation of your own experiences in life. There is no need to go to business school to determine that – unless your teachers can challenge your own experiences, perceptions and approach.

This book is all about these things. It is based on extensive informal study of thousands of different managers in hundreds of organizations over the last 30 years, and by observing carefully those who had an exceptional way with people and who were able, as a consequence, to achieve great results.

Three or four pages are devoted to each of the things you must do to be a great boss. There is no particular logic to the way the pages are strung together and so the book can be dipped into at any point. Inevitably there is a degree of overlap across some of the sections. Each three or four page section will present a challenge to you, even though what is being said might be blatantly obvious. The challenge is to look at yourself and question yourself: 'This is so blatantly obvious I should be doing it. If not, why not?'

One commonly used buzz-word is 'competence' or 'competency'. Organization after organization are establishing training and development programmes based on 'core competencies'. There are even 'sets of competencies' for managers, and, in Britain, MCI has produced a long list of management standards and definitions for various levels of managers. Personally, I find it difficult to relate to much of this. Somehow it lacks life, comes across as incredibly boring, and seems pure textbook stuff. So, I don't know whether the things I write about in this book (the 79 80 things a manager must do) are competencies or not. I would welcome readers' comments on this quandary!

Essentially, this book is a challenge to what is important to you as a reader when you are managing people. It is a 'mind over matter' challenge. If it matters to you and you have a mind to do it, you will do it. Use this book as a golden opportunity to question yourself about the things you do and what is important to you in managing people.

What matters to me, the author, is people. I fundamentally believe that success in business derives from getting the 'people thing' right first. That was a lesson taught to me at the outset of my career when I joined Mars Ltd as a production manager. Mars invested an inordinate amount of time, effort, and energy in managing to get the 'people thing' right. What followed was Mars' continuing success.

This book, effectively, is a reflection of my own beliefs. I believe that success in managing people is all about putting into practice some common-sense basics of life; it is all about challenging yourself on these basics – before you lose sight of them. The concepts are simple, the challenge of applying them is great!

1

Cut the claptrap

Jargon is the language of the ignorant!

Refuse to use any jargon!

A vast industry has sprung up to create an illusion of progress by inventing new words for old practices. Energies are diverted, people are alienated, and efforts are thwarted as managers scramble for definition and interpretation of the new words in a vain attempt to relate them to modern practice.

Get rid of these words! If you use them in your everyday work as a manager you will simply repel your people, who will see you as being divorced from reality and riding high on textbooks.

The problem with using terms like 'empowerment' is that people waste huge amounts of energy trying to understand what the word means. Every single person will have a different interpretation – and this leads to immense division and conflict while people argue it out.

If you want to relate to people (and good management practice is all about this) you need to use simple, clear language that most people understand. You will appear false if you attempt to use artificial management jargon.

It is far better to say 'I'd like to sit down with you this coming Tuesday and have a chat about how things are going' than 'I intend to conduct your annual performance appraisal next week'.

It is far better to say 'I want you to go to New York on my behalf' than 'I am empowering you to go to New York'.

It is far better to say 'I thought I ought to let you know …' than 'I intend to share this piece of information with you'.

JARGON

Briefing groups	Networking
Buying into	Organization development
Change management	Outcomes
Charter	Outward bound training
Clean sheet solutions	Ownership (of ideas, etc.)
Coaching (with the manager as a coach)	Partnership working
Communications	Performance appraisal
Competencies	Performance indicators
Core values	Performance management
Customerizing	Process mapping
Devolvement	Psychometric testing
Downsizing	Quality circles
Empowerment	Re-engineering
Enabling	Sensitivity training
End results	Sharing (of ideas, etc.)
Excellence	Steering groups
Focus groups	Strategic leadership
Globalization	T-groups
Human resources	Targeting
Internal customers	Teamwork
The learning organization	Total Quality Management (TQM)
Liberation management	Transactional Analysis
Management By Objectives (MBO)	Upward appraisal
Merit pay	Vision
Mission	Working parties

(NB: This list is far from exhaustive!)

The trouble with inventing concepts like 'performance appraisal' is that it leads people to assume that everyone's performance can be measured objectively. It is also based on the premise that subjective decisions about people are bad and potentially unfair. By passively accepting the conventional wisdom that 'performance appraisal' (or 'empowerment', or 'teamwork') is 'good' many managers waste time attempting to put these concepts into practice without having questioned the underlying assumptions and premises on which they are based. These assumptions and premises are frequently invalid. For example, the jargon term 'performance pay', or 'merit pay', is based on the discredited assumption that the 'carrot and stick' theory of motivation works.

Similarly, with 'teamwork'. A simple assumption is made that every employee can be slotted into a discrete group of people that can form the basis of excellent leadership and teamwork. It is quite logical, therefore, to invest lots of money into training in 'leadership' and 'teamwork'. The assumption, though, is invalid. In the majority of organizations, people do *not* work in discrete teams. Most people are at the centre of a complex web of relationships extending beyond their immediate boss or the people with whom they work. By abolishing the use of the jargon term 'teamwork', managers can concentrate on more important issues, such as how any one person works together with the other people they need to relate to in everyday work.

The use of jargon attempts to simplify the practice of management into a number of palatable components; it is 'painting by numbers'. The result, though, is unnecessary confusion and potential constraint on the application of common sense. If you want the real thing, get rid of the jargon!

PRINCIPLE:
Mutual understanding.

PRACTICE:
Use, clear, everyday language.
Never use jargon.

2

Abolish all modern people-management techniques

So-called modern management techniques are effectively crutches or strait-jackets for incompetent managers.

In our working lives, there is a definite need for technique. It is important that we devise practical methods to help us manage our finances and, for example, make sensible pricing decisions. We need procedures to analyse market trends and predict sales. It is important that we have techniques for controlling utilization of equipment and for monitoring product quality. We even need business plans and tangible measures of what people produce. We also have to have systems to examine response times and to optimize the logistics of our business in order to achieve speedy and on-time deliveries.

What we *don't* really need are techniques for managing people. During the last 30 years, many managers have attempted to practise alchemy in improving relations and performance at work. It was as if there was some magic technique that could convert ordinary people into highly motivated high performers who could outstrip those of the competition.

THE ALCHEMY OF MODERN MANAGEMENT

- **Performance management techniques (appraisal, performance related pay (PRP), etc.)**
- **Management By Objectives**
- **Quality circles**
- **Total Quality Management**
- **Briefing groups**
- **Focus groups**
- **Sensitivity training**
- **Outward bound training**
- **Team building**
- **Psychometric testing**
- **Assessment centres**
- **Empowerment**
- **Development of core competencies**
- **Organization development**

(examples)

Of course, most ordinary people are capable of high performance. The point is that it is highly unlikely you will achieve it by using any of these pseudo-scientific practices. Most of them have been developed by people posing as experts to create an illusion of modern management practice. There is no indication that organizations that practice this alchemy are any more successful than those that don't. In fact, there is every indication that those that don't are more successful than those that do.

Managing people at work is a complicated task that cannot, and should not, be reduced to mere procedure. The core theme of this book is that managing people is based on a number of common-sense principles that, in reality, are incredibly difficult to put into practice.

You cannot devise procedures for the behaviours and attitudes from which effective working relationships evolve. Furthermore, you cannot devise systems for changing them. The key – as is stressed continually throughout this book – is to challenge the behaviours and attitudes and the principles and practices of yourself and your people, all the time.

What the so-called experts have tried to do during the last 30 years is to convert a number of medieval-type rituals into bureaucratic management techniques based on hierarchical status and privilege.

If both parties find the ritual helpful (for example, the ritual of performance appraisal) then perhaps they should continue the practice. Furthermore, if you are attracted to a special technique to help you challenge your own principles and practices, you should use it. In other words, while there is no real need for these techniques and while some of them are based on false premises, it could just so happen that one or two people find them helpful. Even this writer cannot be that absolute!

This said, the mistake is to *impose* these techniques. It is common sense for any boss to regularly communicate with his or her people, if you find it helpful to label this as a 'briefing group' and systematize the process, then do so, but don't *force* the label and the system on everyone else – it won't make them better managers. In practice, if you are a great boss, you will be communicating with your people regularly and you won't need to label what, in effect, you do naturally as a 'briefing group'. If you're *not* a great boss and need such a system and a label to help you along, then use the system and the label, *but* don't delude yourself that it is the system and the label that will make you and your people more effective (that is the delusion of the alchemist). None of these systems are magic wands. The solution to improved effectiveness must always come from within yourself. These solutions are invariably based on the application of common-sense principles. So, you must ask yourself why you need the systems and labels when the solution is a natural one and well within your own capability. The danger is that the system becomes either a crutch on which managers become dependent or a strait-jacket that constrains them. My preference would be to abolish all these pseudo-scientific techniques and let managers get on and manage without hindrance and constraint from the centre.

Organizations should concentrate on *what* people achieve and not interfere with *how* they achieve it, rather, they should provide support in this process.

PRINCIPLE:
There are no simple effective techniques for managing people.

No such techniques should ever be imposed.

PRACTICE:
Examine any techniques you currently use for managing your people. Retain those you find helpful; abolish the rest.

3

Use your common sense

The basics of being a great boss are common sense and have been around for centuries.

The trouble with many organizations today is that they do not trust their people to use their heads, to use common sense. So, they prescribe bureaucratic procedures for doing many basic things. As mentioned in the previous section, these so-called modern procedures for people management should be abolished. Instead, organizations should rely on the *nous* of their managers and people. The problem with overemphasis on a prescriptive approach to people management is that people lose track of common sense and forget to apply it. They are railroaded down tracks that force them to do it one way as opposed to a more sensible way. They are forced into briefing groups, then fail to communicate at other times; they are forced into performance appraisal systems, then fail to provide feedback at other times when a person's performance is exceptional or lamentable. It is almost as if managers today are frightened of doing anything sensible in managing people unless it has been prescribed and labelled by the organization as a 'system'.

To me, it is common sense to say 'Thank you' for a job done well. You don't need a system for this. Regrettably, though, too many managers neglect to say 'Thank you' at the right time, relying solely on a bureaucratic performance review procedure for a rather formalized expression of appreciation.

We are taught common sense as children. We are taught how to cross a road. We are taught not to talk to strangers. We are taught to be polite and courteous and to say 'Thank you' to a kind aunt who brings a present. We are taught to help around the house, to avoid touching hot pans and boiling kettles. We are taught to share our sweets and not to play in our neighbours' gardens. We are taught respect and are expected to be trusted and not to steal.

Few families, if any, would bother to write this into a 'manual of family rules and procedures'. In fact, the idea would seem ridiculous to most of us. Yet, the ridiculous thing is that many organizations write up these common-sense things into rule books and procedures.

Senior executives seem to have an intrinsic fear that their managers and their people will not do the right thing, will not say 'Thank you', will not help each other out, will not communicate, will not act in a safe way.

The paradox is that while good management practice is based on the application of common sense (like listening to people, like saying 'Thank you' for a job done well) it is blatantly obvious that common sense is frequently *not* applied by many managers. The reason is that common sense cannot stand alone; it has to be challenged continually. Unless you do so common sense becomes distorted sense. As we saw, it is common sense not to smoke, not to eat too much, not to consume too much alcohol, to take regular exercise, but few of us challenge ourselves sufficiently to follow these common-sense rules.

We all have a common sense of what it is right and proper to do. What is much more difficult is to put it into practice. The basic principles of management are no more than common sense (caring for your people, putting yourself out for your customers, etc.). They are basically simple ideas and easy to understand. The difficult thing is putting them into practice, and that's the challenge. The answer is not to turn practice into a procedure because this carries the huge risk of obscuring the principle. The answer is to ensure that we all *internalize* these basic principles of management and *believe* in them because they are fundamentally important to us and the way we go about our work. We then need to continually challenge ourselves on how we put these principles into practice – constantly learning from our mistakes, constantly searching for improvement,

9

constantly redefining what we mean by common sense. Procedures cannot do that for us.

DON'T WE KNOW ALL THIS? IT'S COMMON SENSE!

'It came home to me during a recent visit to the USA and a trip to a major theme park which has London-style double-decker buses to take you around the lake and stop off at various attractions. I had spent my student days in London and was used to hopping on to the platform of a moving No. 19 bus at the Angel and lurching up the stairs as the bus accelerated away. In the American theme park it was different. Before the bus moved off a conductor passed around to ensure every passenger was seated. The conductor then put a rope across the platform of the bus to prevent anyone falling off. A safety announcement was then made telling people not to stand until the bus had stopped. The bus then proceeded to travel at no more than five miles an hour around the theme park. Having got off the bus, my family and I entered one of the attractions. There was a moving walkway. As we stepped on to the moving walkway, there was another safety announcement telling us to hold on to the handrail, not to run, and, later, to inform us we were approaching the end of the moving walkway and to take care in stepping off. All the time I kept on saying to myself, "Why are these people telling me all this. It's common sense".'

This book is based on common sense. None of the principles underpinning the 80 things you must do to be a great boss should be any surprise to you. The danger is that you lose sight of them in pursuit of your organization's *interpretation* of what you must do. Far better to develop your *own* interpretation and put *that* into practice. In other words, you must be yourself rather than let your employer define what you should be. That's why large hierarchical organizations are proving to be less and less successful in this day and age. Such organizations attempt to condition their people into a particular mind-set of what they should be, constraining them from being themselves. Most people, when allowed to be themselves will act on common sense, take up the challenges, and drive themselves forwards to great success. There is nothing magical about becoming successful, and you can't devise procedures for it!

PRINCIPLE:
The practice of managing people is based on common sense.

PRACTICE:
You have to challenge yourself regularly on how you apply common sense.

4

Treat people as human beings

Equality of opportunity is all about recognizing each other as human beings.

There is a danger that we forget that people are human beings. All we see is a label that brings to mind a prejudicial stereotype, so we react to the label in a way that anticipates the behaviour we expect of that stereotype; we fail to react to the human being. It leads to unthinking discrimination and causes immense problems.

Unpeel the layers of status, position, and circumstance and there are many fundamental similarities. We all have feelings. We all have views. We all have a little more intelligence than others credit us with.

What differentiates us is our clothes, our language and accent, our experience, our skills, our background, and our beliefs. None of that should mark us out for differential treatment.

As a great boss you need to forget *who* people are, and treat them for *what* they are. Whether they are a minister in the Government, chief executive, pop star, trade union official, personnel manager, office cleaner, or security guard they should all merit the same treatment.

I have countless stories of senior people refusing to talk to junior people because of rank, of senior people treating junior people as if they knew nothing. Being patronizing, looking down on people, displaying arrogance, pulling rank - are the marks of a very poor boss.

Treating people like human beings is all about respect. We all have an intrinsic worth that needs to be recognized and valued. The most debilitating experience at work is when you feel devalued. That experience can result from the colour of your skin, the state of your physique, the way you talk, the rank you hold in the organization.

People hate to be put down, yet many bosses inadvertently do it all the time. They ignore certain classes of people who then feel rejected and let down. They fail to listen to people at a lower hierarchical level irrespective of the value of what they have to say. These people are led to believe that they are inferior and inadequate.

Treating people like human beings is to take a genuine interest in everyone. It is not to make assumptions about individuals because of any label attached to them. It is not being prejudicial.

Much of our behaviour is subconscious. We are unaware of the signals we send out, even of what we do. We are frequently unaware of the impact we have on others. We communicate our prejudices without realizing. We go to talk to the supervisor and neglect to say 'Hello' to the clerk standing alongside. We pass by a couple of messengers without acknowledging their presence. We open the door for a director but fail to do so for the young apprentice from the factory. We tend to automatically assume that a person is going to behave in a way consistent with the stereotypical image we have of that type of person. We then allow our prejudice to be reinforced when the person does behave that way, neatly forgetting all the instances when they don't.

There is a truism that goes: 'treat a person the way you'd like to be treated yourself'. Analyse how you like to be treated – the courtesies, the respect, the praise, the openness and honesty, the friendly, warm manner, the sharing of confidences – then treat everyone else the same way, whoever they might be.

Being the boss makes no difference. As human beings your people are the equal of you. They should have the same entitlements in terms of expression and treatment; standards of courtesy should not vary according to status.

TREAT PEOPLE EQUALLY

Irrespective of:

- status
- job type
- religion
- country/town of birth
- colour of skin
- gender
- style of dress/appearance
- reputation
- whether they report to you or you report to them
- physique
- capability
- accent
- attitude towards you
- age

Treating people like human beings is about resisting making value judgements. Value people, yes, but try not to make value judgements about them because certain individuals and groups of people do not conform to your way of life. Your way might be right for you but in no way can you judge it to be the best way for others. There is no best way to live. All we can do is make judgements of what is best for us and leave others to make their own judgements. We have to respect that.

The great boss will treat their people as equal human beings, not as inferiors who have yet to make it.

PRINCIPLE:
Equality of opportunity.

Equality of treatment.

PRACTICE:
Forget who people are (status, rank, etc.).

Do not differentiate between people because of pre-set labels attached to them (race, association/ club, religion).

Treat everyone the same (speak to all).

5

Clarify your expectations

Expect nothing if your expectations are not clear.

People need to know what is in your mind, what you expect of them.

The worst bosses are those who are totally unpredictable, who want one thing one minute and the opposite the next. They are the bosses who are forever being accused of changing the goalposts, of sending out conflicting signals, of blowing with the wind, of reacting to their own bosses, and not having a mind of their own.

Therein lies the key. You must be very clear what you want of your people and communicate these expectations to them. You have to make up your mind about what standards you want them to attain, about what latitude to give them in their own decision making, about how they ought to behave with one another as well as with you.

Expectations are not solely concerned with the accomplishment of major objectives; they have a lot to do with the routines of everyday working life. The best bosses expect their people to be punctual: to turn up at meetings on time, to arrive at work at the agreed hour, to never keep anyone waiting. The best bosses expect their people to return telephone calls, to reply to letters, to keep their promises. They expect courtesy and the demonstration of respect to all. They expect their people to speak up as well as listen carefully. They expect openness and honesty.

These expectations are no more than common sense. Thus, they do not need to be written down and turned into bureaucratic procedures, but they do need to be clear in each person's mind. Without that clarity, standards will erode, disorganization and muddle will set in.

Clarity of expectation, therefore, must be reinforced by actual practice and real demonstration. A great boss will not tolerate lateness, unless there is an exceptional reason. Discourtesy and lack of respect will also be seen to be unacceptable. This does not mean that transgressors have to be punished, but, more likely, that a firm but kind word in the ear is required.

The best opportunity to spell out these expectations is when you first take over as the boss. You don't have to impose your expectations, all you need to do is to agree them with your new group of people. The process of agreement will, in effect, clarify the expectations.

Some people like to have a 'code of conduct' and there is no harm in this if it is found to be helpful.

Expectations also extend into work objectives and a clarity of purpose. Any one person needs to know what is expected of him or her in the job. Unfortunately, job descriptions are rarely of help in this connection. As stressed in other sections of this book the key expectation should be focused on *what* a person has to achieve in the job. A great boss will expect a person to decide *how* best to go about achieving this. A further expectation is that the person will come to the boss if help is needed, or any further support required, or to inform the boss (before the event) that certain targets are not being met and remedial action is being taken.

Expectations are always mutual and as a boss you will need to clarify with your people what they expect of you. When you take over as the boss, it is worth having a mutual discussion to clarify your expectations of each other. But even if you have been the boss for 20 years, it is not too late to sit down with your people and take stock of the expectations you have of each other and review and develop them.

Failure to define and agree expectations will reflect badly on you as a boss. You will be seen as weak, indecisive, lacking in direction, muddled, and confused. Conversely, by clarifying expectations you will enhance your credibility, you will be respected. As mentioned above, the process need not be formal, but can be conducted informally. In fact, it can be an evolutionary process, established and reinforced by your own actions in certain situations. You can start off by assuming high standards and then respond in a helpful, constructive way when people fall short. They will soon learn what your expectations are of them.

The importance of clarifying expectations should not be under-estimated. Without a clear set of expectations, people go off in different directions, it makes them feel vulnerable, uncertain, suspicious. While people should be allowed a high degree of discretion in *how* they go about their work, they do need to work within certain boundaries of what is acceptable to you, the boss, and the organization as a whole. Without a definition and understanding of these boundaries, people go astray. Your job, therefore, is to define the boundaries within which your people have the freedom to operate. That is what clarifying expectations is all about.

You should also expect *a lot* of your people (this subject is covered in a later section).

PRINCIPLE:
People need to know what you expect of them as a boss. You also need to know what they expect of you.

PRACTICE:
Sit down with your people and review your expectations of each other and agree them. Prepare a simple check-list beforehand as a basis for your discussion.

6

Listen and take action

A failure to listen is not only a mark of disrespect but also incredibly foolish.

The people who tend to get on in this world are those who tend to be assertive, have a lot of drive, believe in themselves, persevere at all costs, and know how to overcome adversity – all admirable qualities. The danger is that, in developing these qualities, these people develop an inherent weakness. They fail to listen, they fail to take advice. They become victims of their own success, believing that, because they have been successful in the past, they must be right in everything they say and do now.

There is enough evidence of this failing all around. You only have to study the downfall of Margaret Thatcher to find one excellent example. Other examples can be found in one of my previous books (*Incredible Bosses*, McGraw-Hill, 1990), which dealt at length with this type of problem. However, one of the classics on the subject is Norman Dixon's *On the Psychology of Military Incompetence* (Jonathan Cape, 1976). This book should be essential reading for all managers. A brief extract from Chapter 11 follows.

THE FALL OF SINGAPORE

'Why did General Percival ignore the urgent advice of his subordinate, Brigadier Simson, and of his superior, General Wavell, to implement these defences? ...

'... What General Percival shared with other, earlier, military incompetents were passivity and courtesy, rigidity and obstinacy, procrastination, gentleness and dogmatism.'

One has to differentiate between *listening* and *hearing*. There are three keys to this. The first is to understand what the other person is trying to say. The second is not to reject what the person is saying because it conflicts with your own views. The third is to take action on what is being said.

Too many managers merely go through the motions of listening – reverting to clichés: 'It goes in one ear and out the other'.

To listen effectively, you have to forget yourself. You have to 'put yourself in the other person's shoes'. You have to get inside what they are trying to tell you, what they really mean. All this has to be underpinned by a healthy degree of trust and respect. You cannot listen to people you do not trust, and you have to respect that they have more expertise, more wisdom on the subject in hand than you do. By allowing people to talk, by trying to understand through effective listening, you can often help them find the solution to their own problems. Having a sympathetic and understanding listener enables you to clear your mind, to untangle the confusions that are riddling you.

Failure to listen is endemic in large, traditional hierarchies with authoritarian bosses. There is an implicit assumption that a person of higher status must always be right, with a resultant fear of challenging that person. This is the main reason that many organizations are being turned upside down today.

TYPICAL! THEY LISTEN BUT TAKE NO ACTION!

'For nine months we've had a broken window in our laboratory. I've chased building maintenance countless times but they always seem to be too busy with more important things. It is always "mañana"! Our Director came round three months ago and asked how things were going. I pointed out the broken window. He nodded and said "I will get it fixed, don't worry".

'That was three months ago. It's still not been fixed.'

Listen carefully to your people. They probably know more than you think they do. They probably have better solutions to problems than you.

When you listen to people, take notes. Then, take action.

Listening is not the same as agreeing with every one. That is impossible. The action you take will always be to give serious consideration to what a person says. Sometimes, however, the end result is that you will disagree. The action you take then is to go back to the person and explain, in a courteous way, why the decision has gone against him or her.

The greatest bosses, the greatest leaders, the greatest people are great listeners.

PRINCIPLE:
To listen is to learn. To learn is to make progress.

To listen is to show respect. The more people you respect, the greater your progress will be.

PRACTICE:
Always let people finish what they are saying.

Explore what a person is saying to make sure you completely understand.

Don't let your own prejudices get in the way.

Take notes, otherwise you will forget.

Then, take action on what the person has said.

7

Provide direction

You have to know where you are taking your people.

People need to know in which direction they are going. It is one thing they cannot decide for themselves. Ideally the organization will have long-term goals for success and these have to be subdivided into achievable targets that every individual, every section, and every department can shoot at.

One of the jobs you have as a boss, therefore, is to translate these long-term goals into specific targets to be achieved by your people. But, this is not enough. Over and above what the *organization* requires, you will need to decide what *you* want out of the section or department. It is not sufficient just to react to the demands of the organization. An excellent boss will need to convince senior executives that the section (or department) has additional value that can be exploited to the benefit of all. In other words, there is a continual process of justifying your existence, of selling what you do. Senior executives change frequently, their requirements change. Furthermore, the market changes. Great bosses will do as much as they can to stop these changes threatening the jobs of their people. They will not let destiny control their futures, preferring to control their own destiny. To achieve that requires manoeuvring into the best position in the market-place, internal or external, such that there is an ongoing if not growing demand for the services and products provided by your section.

This is all to do with direction. Great bosses can and should take direction from their employers. However, they should provide additional direction in terms of what they personally want to achieve at work. This cannot be defined by senior bosses who are not always in the best position to know the potential of any particular unit.

Therefore, it is critically important that once every few months you sit down with your people and create a picture (the jargon word is 'vision') of how you see the future. By bringing this picture into focus, you will be able to provide a clear direction of the way forward for your unit. In the first instance, you might need to go away for a couple of days to really thrash out the direction you want to go in.

Once established, you must always carry this picture in your mind. It should be a simple picture of the future, like getting to the moon, or winning the cup final, or writing a best-seller – a picture of success you can clearly visualize. Furthermore, it should represent some challenge which you and your people are going to derive immense satisfaction from meeting. It can be a picture relating to exceptional standards of service to customers, of continued innovation on the product side, of the highest possible levels of quality, of increasing demand on your services in the market-place, of providing the most sought after advice in the organization and elsewhere.

Whatever the direction you establish, it will have to be quantified in terms of budgets. In pursuing your direction you will need to put cases forward for investment, if appropriate, or for major changes that are going to have an impact on the rest of the organization (this process of planning is covered in a later section).

Having established a clear direction and a plan for pursuing it, your job as a boss is to ensure that every single person for whom you are responsible knows where they fit in. In other words, you need to provide direction to every person in the group.

People might be able to decide how best to get there, but you have to decide where they are going. You might even have to change the interim destination from time to time if problems arise.

One of the unfortunate buzz-words of recent times is 'empowerment'. Managers have become very confused over the meaning and how 'empowerment' can be practised. The critical differentiation is that you cannot empower people to decide *what* they are going to achieve, only *how* they are going to achieve it.

Deciding 'what people have to achieve' is the process of *giving direction*. A boss takes accountability for pursuing this direction and ensuring everyone arrives at the ultimate destination, whether it be a 99.9 per cent reliability on deliveries, the best productivity levels in the industry, the best-trained group of people in the profession, the friendliest customer service imaginable, innovative new products coming on stream regularly, or the highest technical capability anywhere.

Create a spare moment and sit down and reflect on what you are there for as a boss. Are you really clear what you want to achieve? Does this really embrace what the organization requires of you, plus a little more? Does it offer the best prospects for the future for you and your people?

CONFLICTING SIGNALS

'The problem with this company is that we keep on getting conflicting signals about what is required. One minute there is an initiative on customer service, the next minute it is TQM. Then all that seems to be forgotten about and we are all into cost-cutting. Then we are into some new style of performance management which central personnel have invented. It goes on and on. We have new initiatives coming out of our ears. We just don't know where we are going. We waste a lot of time on these different fads and it distracts us from our real work.'

Never delude yourself that your hands are tied behind your back by your all-powerful employers: there is always scope for putting your own personal thumb-print on the direction of the unit you manage. Gone are the days when autocratic directors told everyone in the organization what to do, what to think. To survive today you have to make your own way into the future, creating your own direction off the back of what the organization wants. Your people require it of you – they see it as your prime role.

PRINCIPLE:
The importance of knowing where you are going.

PRACTICE:
Regularly review the direction of your unit and ensure everyone knows the way you and they are going.

8

Be unconventional, be unique!

Convention constrains while unconventional practice is the source of all progress.

You should never do things differently just for the sake of it. However, doing something differently is the only way to make progress.

People who try to follow convention effectively follow the rest. They try to do everything the same. Besides being boring, this is no way to compete. Competition is all about doing things better – and that means doing things differently.

This said, convention does have its place when we talk of the norms of civilized behaviour. It has its place at work in terms of how we relate to each other, for example through friendly conventional greetings and a genuine word of thanks. Convention, therefore, applies when we do not wish to change accepted good practice.

But, the world of business is all about change, is all about establishing a uniqueness in the minds of your customers. There is no option, therefore, but to use an unconventional approach to effect change and develop that uniqueness. A conventional approach can never secure that. So, be unconventional! Exceed expectations. Surprise your customers with imaginative moves. Excite your people with new and creative initiatives.

UNCONVENTIONAL PRACTICE

- Let your staff decide their own salaries
- Get your staff to train your customers
- Get your customers to train your people
- Implement totally flexible working hours (no paper, no records, complete trust)
- Be completely open and honest with your customers
- Be completely open and honest with your people
- Abolish all privileges (cars, parking, travel, titles, etc.)
- Reduce paper by 90 per cent
- Get rid of performance appraisals
- Ban suits and ties from your office and explain to your customers
- Reward mistakes and failures as soon as the lessons have been learned
- Do something very unusual with your people (outside work)
- Do something very unusual with your customers (outside work)
- Get your customers to invent new products/services for you
- Nail a scrap board to your office wall and encourage people to stick Post-it notes on it saying whatever they want, giving prizes for the most original items
- Write a book of your people's achievements. Show photographs in it
- Make sure each of your people comes up with one new imaginative idea at least once a year, and ensure that it is implemented

Create a climate in which creativity is encouraged and rewarded. Give careful consideration to whatever ideas your people come up with. Never reject anything out of hand. Try things out, experiment, run pilot exercises or trials.

You also need to be unconventional in your own behaviour. People love colourful bosses who are slightly out of the ordinary, who put their feet on the desk, loosen their ties, wear bright yellow socks and who come out with the unusual, unexpected phrase. Too many bosses are bores who conform to the grey suit, grey face stereotype.

UNCONVENTIONAL PRACTICE

Approximately 3000 people attended the annual convention of the Institute of Directors at the Royal Albert Hall, London, in April 1993. Of these, it is estimated that 2000 were men, of whom 1999 were wearing suits and ties.

There was one notable exception. And he was the keynote speaker, Richard Branson. He did not wear a tie to give his address, and, in the middle of it, he removed his jacket. He also spoke using the language of common sense and sprinkled his talk with certain idiomatic phrases not normally heard at such conventions.

Inject colour into your people's working lives by going about your everyday routines – well, in a non-routine way! Make the coffee, sweep the floor, empty the waste-paper basket, speak in French, bring in chocolate cake, let your hair grow long, cut it short. Tell stories. Show snaps of your family. Bring in a vase of flowers. Take photographs of people working and enlarge them.

Just do something different – it is so boring otherwise. Your customers will benefit in the end.

PRINCIPLE:
Unconventional practice is the source of progress.

PRACTICE:
Identify and challenge all conventional practices.
Can we do it differently and better?

9

Hold your people to account

Accountability is an elusive commodity.

When you work in an organization where mistakes are punished, good ideas suppressed and bosses don't listen, people avoid accountability. They prefer to push decisions on to others. Frequently, this means pushing decisions upwards to the highest possible level. Hierarchical bosses welcome this, it enhances their status, they feel more powerful because people have to come to them. Regrettably the consequence is frequently failure. The decision-making processes in the organization become overheated and critical decisions are often delayed or not made at all. Frequently the decisions are poor, recommendations having been processed and sanitized through layer and layer of the organization's bureaucracy.

Common sense dictates that decisions are best made by those who have the real knowledge and experience of the impact of that decision on the business. In other words, decisions are best made by the people who have to implement them. For example, a decision on how best to satisfy a customer with an unusual requirement is best made by a person as close to the point of service delivery as possible. That often means people at the front line.

So far the theory is great. You can describe it with any buzz-word you like – delegation, devolvement, empowerment, enabling, decentralization, and participation come to mind immediately.

While the theory is great, the actual practice is actually incredibly difficult. To push decision making towards the front line requires a giant leap of faith. It means having immense trust in the capability of your people to make decisions traditionally made by yourself as a boss.

It also means holding your people to account for their decisions. Accountability means being responsible for a certain decision, it means being answerable for the consequences of that decision. It means having assessed all the risks involved before taking that decision (decisions where no risk is involved are easy). It means ensuring that effective consultation takes place beforehand and clear communication afterwards. It means owning up to poor decisions and accepting failure when it occurs.

Many people shy away from this, having been inured through deference to the dictatorial decisions of autocratic bosses who would insist on making every tiny decision.

On the more positive side, holding people to account enables them to obtain more job satisfaction, to attain more control over what they are paid to deliver, and to relate the fruits of their labours directly to their decisions.

'I'LL TRUST YOU WITH A $35 000 DECISION, BUT NOT WITH A £50 ONE!'

'When I was in the airline business we had a manager whose responsibility, among others, was to negotiate contract room rates for air crews staying in different hotels around the world. One day he returned from California having negotiated a three-dollar reduction of our room rates in Los Angeles. This amounted to a saving of upwards of $35 000 in a full year.

On his return he found a memo on his desk from the Finance Director dictating that no manager could hire in a temporary secretary without permission from a Director.

He came to me, absolutely furious. "I've just returned from the States", he told me, "I've saved the company $35 000. My secretary is ill and I'm not permitted to make a decision to spend fifty pounds to hire in a temporary to type up an urgent report that you, my boss, requires!" '

Holding people to account will have a cathartic effect on any organization. It clears away much of the muddle and bureaucracy that occurs when too many decisions are forced upwards. It forces people to think for themselves and think through the consequences of their own actions.

Holding people to account does not mean elaborate job descriptions and reams of paper spelling out exactly what decisions they can or cannot make. In fact, it means abolishing job descriptions. Holding people to account means attaining a clear understanding of what has to be achieved and then allowing them to get on and achieve it, holding them accountable for the result.

You should hold people to account for *what* they achieve, not *how* they achieve it (within reason). Too many bosses interfere in the 'how' bit, dictating 'how' people should go about their jobs.

The critical area is money. In simple terms, people should agree budgets for achieving certain results and then be given total discretion on how to spend those budgets in pursuit of these goals. If they are foolish enough to spend their budgets unwisely and the results are not achieved, then they should obviously be held to account for this.

It is important, therefore, that you sit back and reflect on the *way* you hold your people accountable, and *what* you hold them accountable for. There is no doubt that the more accountability you allow people, the better their performance will be.

PRINCIPLE:
Trusting people to make decisions.

Getting people to answer for their decisions.

PRACTICE:
Ensure that there is total clarity and understanding with your people on what has to be achieved.

Let them get on and achieve it, and ensure they report back to you at appropriate times.

10

Push for your people

People will never push in the direction you want unless you push for them.

Get your people promoted. Get them the best training. Get them new experiences. Fight for their pay increases. Fight to improve their environment. Fight their corner when they're under attack. Promote their achievements. Wave their flag for them. Take on their case on their behalf.

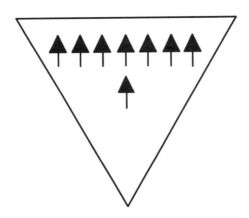

Conversely, never fight your own people. You can argue, you can disagree, you can feel bad about each other occasionally, but never ever fight your people.

The whole history of management is riddled with 'us and them' differences, where management are seen as separate from workers, where opposing vested interests are the order of the day. The lesson is that such differences generate a climate of distrust and extensive industrial unrest.

As a boss, you are an important and intrinsic part of the group for which you are responsible as manager. You should never consider yourself separate from the group. Do not fear those above you who might accuse you of being 'one of the boys' (or 'girls'), or 'going native', or 'someone who's on *their* side as opposed to *our* side as management'. In any organization everyone should be on the *same* side. That means that you should be on the side of the people who deliver the results at the front line for the organization.

It means that you have to push hard to create a situation whereby your people have the optimum conditions to produce the best results. It means pushing hard to ensure that their own personal interests are looked after. People will be motivated when they are conscious that the boss is pushing to create opportunities to develop their careers, to get them better working conditions, to present them with more exciting challenges.

Not surprisingly, when people feel you are pushing for *them*, they will push for *you*. They will give you that little bit extra when required, they will put themselves out for you, they will try a little harder. They won't ask anything in return because they will know that you will always be doing your best for them.

Tonight, reflect on what you have done for your people recently. In what way have you pushed for them, supported their cause?

PRINCIPLE:
Fairness. Those who you push for will push for you.

PRINCIPLE:
Find out what the most pressing needs of your people are and attempt to address them on their behalf.

11

Go home

Don't devalue your home by working excessive hours.

I once worked for a company in which I had to make large numbers of people redundant, including some of my director colleagues. I had senior executives crying in my office as I handed them their redundancy notices. Some of them had worked for the company for over 30 years, they had given their everything to the firm, they had been totally loyal. And then recession hit the industry and their jobs were no longer wanted. What price loyalty? They had totally neglected their families in favour of working excessive hours for the company, only to be fired 30 years later. It is a harsh world.

I cannot remember bringing up my son and daughter by my first marriage. I think I know the reason why. I was never home. I was a workaholic. I left home before the kids got up, I arrived home after they had gone to bed. I saw them at weekends, and at weekends I tended to work.

It is all to do with personal values. Family is important, but it is the family that frequently gets neglected as people indulge their passion for work. For some managers, work is an easy escape from an unhappy marriage, but you cannot reconstruct a relationship when you are never with your partner.

Furthermore, excessive hours present a bad example. People watch you. The longer you work, the more guilty they become if they don't emulate you. The rot sets in. People become fearful of leaving before the boss, of arriving after him or her. Extending the hours at work rarely means extra productivity or better results. Frequently, it means inefficiency and unnecessary intrusion into the detail of other people's work.

Work should be enjoyable and it is logical to justify the extra hours on this basis. But being with your family should also be enjoyable and also justify a reasonable proportion of your time, day in and day out.

The world is hostile. It is the survival of the fittest. Some would argue, therefore, that long hours are necessary to survive. What survives? The family? The marriage? The job?

It is not impossible to strike a balance. Long hours will inevitably be necessary on many occasions during one's career. But, more frequently, they will be unnecessary. We all have a tendency to create unnecessary work to fill the space.

The other major consideration is health. Not only your health, but the health of the organization. With rare exceptions, the longer you work, the more tired you become. The more tired you become, the more prone you are to making bad decisions.

There were days when I got in at 7.30 a.m. and worked through meeting after meeting until 7.00 p.m. only then to face a huge pile of papers waiting for me at the end of the day. I would find I could not assimilate the material. Being mentally exhausted, I could not comprehend the recommendations in this paper and the statements in that. The various reports seemed to have no meaning. Words would not register, my mind would wander, I could not concentrate. Yet, decisions had to be made. So I would defer them until first thing the following morning. With new energies and a fresh mind, everything I couldn't take in the previous evening suddenly became clear. I found decisions much easier to make then.

Many executives have a deep-rooted psychological fear of doing anything other than work. Beside the guilt feeling about not working, they feel they are going to miss out on important things and that crucial tasks will not be carried out or that they will not be completely up to date.

It is easy to prove that the world goes on much the same if you get in a little later and leave a little earlier. Somehow, the same amount of work gets done. Somehow, you get a little more efficient. You will discover that what you used to do in 11 hours you can do in 9.

Try going home earlier and spending more time with your family.

You will be amazed to find that the company does not go bankrupt, that profits do not deteriorate, that things do not remain undone. In fact, you will find that your people look happier, that they are fresher, and produce better results.

A basic tenet in this book is that to care for your customers you have to care for your people. You cannot be caring for them if you set a bad example that they feel obliged to follow. Persistently working long hours *is* a bad example.

Life is more than work, and for people to work effectively they must have life beyond work. Encourage it. Send people home early. Frown on those who stay late day in and day out. Never imply that someone who works 'nine to five' is not committed. Never make people feel guilty if they arrive on time and go home on time. Try to develop an ethos in which it is accepted that you should have your desk clear by 5.30 p.m. – and that not to have done so is a result of inefficiency and poor organization.

Go home, take exercise, sit down and chat with your wife, husband or partner, play with your kids. Even get up to date with the latest fashion in television viewing.

PRINCIPLE:
The importance of family, of relaxation.

PRACTICE:
Discipline yourself to work (at least three days a week) the same 'official' hours that employees are contracted to work.

If you currently work excessive hours, set yourself a target to spend at least five hours more per week at home.

12

Be generous

Your people will measure you by your generosity.

There is a myth that management is an exact science, that you are paid for exactly what you contribute, that work is measured down to the last calorie expended. It leads to a frame of mind where *everything* is negotiated – where a simple change in operating routine justifies an extra allowance, where you don't work a minute longer than necessary.

The myth leads to a mentality that everything can be quantified in terms of costs that have to be reduced. People are seen as commodities to be used and disposed of as necessary. All other elements of the business are seen the same way. Work thus becomes a bargaining process. People give their bare minimum and, in return, their employers pay the bare minimum.

Mercifully this myth is a relic of the bad old days of industrial unrest and is becoming less and less prevalent, but remnants still remain in the minds of many managers.

To motivate people you have to be generous. As people's perceptions vary, an exact line cannot be drawn between generosity and meanness. You must, therefore, err on the side of generosity whenever deciding what to give your people – whether it be a pay increase or just buying a round of drinks.

Such generosity should never be part of a bargain – you should never expect anything in return. In reality, you will receive a lot in return. The probability is that if you are generous with your people, they will be generous, too. A minority will exploit your generosity, but you will soon learn and handle them accordingly.

Never hesitate, therefore, to spend money (within reason) on your people. Sometimes it will be the organization's money. At other times it will be your own money.

One of the sacrifices you have to make as a boss is that you cannot claim everything on expenses. Certain expenses – like buying the first round of drinks, like sending out cards at Christmas, like sending flowers to someone who's sick – just have to be borne out of your own pocket. If you attempt to claim these items on expenses, people will sooner or later find out and judge you to be insincere.

Sacrifice is the wrong word – it should not be seen as a pain. Ideally, if you are that noble, you should see it is as a privilege to give something back to your people. You are paid more than them, but they work incredibly hard for you. The least you can do is dip your hand into your pocket occasionally and spend some money on them.

GENEROSITY

- **Always buy the first round of drinks**
- **Err on the side of generosity (make the increase a little more than they expected)**
- **Always pay for the meal**
- **Always pay for the taxi**
- **Give generously whenever there's a whip round**
- **Be generous in praise**
- **If in doubt give, don't take**
- **Try hard to say 'yes' to requests**
- **Give extra time off**
- **Seize opportunities to send presents**
- **Send cards on important occasions**

Generosity is about your own set of values including how you value your people. There are too many mean-minded people around who consciously avoid expenditure. They develop manoeuvres to hang back when the group approaches the bar, to be away from the table when the bill arrives, to be unavailable when there's a 'whip round'. These people are soon seen for what they are. As a boss, you cannot afford to be one of them. It is false economy to save a few pounds by not indulging your people occasionally. Such resistance breeds dissent.

Take pleasure in giving. The rule is equally applicable at work as it is at home. As we progress through life, we realize that little pleasure comes from taking. There has been too much emphasis on taking and not enough on giving. The opportunity starts with you as boss.

And, it is not just giving generously to your people – giving generously to your customers is just as important. The 110 per cent rule should apply here. Always give your customers 10 per cent more than they expected. Be generous with them. Never argue about the last penny – just give it away!

By generating a 'giving' culture, you will experience no end of success.

PRINCIPLE:
Giving generously without expectation of return.

PRACTICE:
Seize every opportunity to spend money on your people.

13

Give instant feedback

Without feedback we all go off course.

People hate to be uncertain about what you, the boss, are thinking. They want to know how you feel about their work, about what's going on in the company as a whole. They want you to give them helpful and constructive feedback at the appropriate time.

None of us is that perfect that we are not ineffective at times, that we don't put a foot wrong, that we don't misinterpret what is said, that we don't start shooting off in the wrong direction.

Feedback is the essence of effective communication. It is also essential for effectiveness at work.

In the normal course of conversation, it is often helpful to feed back to people a summary of what you think they have just said. Unless you know them really well, never assume that you completely understand what has been said. More problems are created at work than anything else as a result of misunderstandings over what has been said. It is not only *what* has been said, but *how* it is said, too. British people are exceptionally skilled at loading their words with undertones and overtones to deflect from the literal meaning of what they say. If you are unsure about what a person is getting at, or if there is any doubt in your mind at all about what is being said, then attempt to summarize and feed back to the person what you think has been said.

But, it is not only through conversation that giving instant feedback is helpful. It is also important to give feedback on how you see people working. The danger with a formal performance appraisal system is that it tends to become a pseudo-scientific substitute practice for what is basically common sense – an exchange of views about a person's effectiveness.

Inevitably, in this age of equality, it is critical that you encourage your people to give you feedback on your own approach. Just because you are the boss doesn't mean to say that you don't occasionally get things wrong, don't occasionally go off course, or don't occasionally say things that confuse people. Encourage your people to speak their mind, to let you know what they're thinking – about you and your work. If you suffer from halitosis, insist that your people tell you. If you inadvertently make people feel small, or fail to listen to what they say, or, what's worse, fail to take action on a promise (simply because you forgot), then it is critical that they let you know.

WHEN THE SYSTEM SAYS YOU CAN'T, USE COMMON SENSE

'In June, three months after I took over as Personnel Director, I informed my managers that I would like to undertake an informal appraisal of their performance. One of my managers reacted rather negatively to this. He had been around a long time. In fact, he was the guy who had devised the company's formal performance appraisal system.

"You cannot appraise us now," he told me, "we always carry out appraisals in November and it's only June. Furthermore the policy says that before you can appraise someone you have to be in the job 12 months and you've only been here three months." Furthermore it's not permitted to use a blank piece of paper as you intend. You have to use the four-page form which everyone uses.

I stared at him almost in total disbelief. After all, he purported to be a personnel professional. "I think I owe it to you," I told him "to give you some feedback about how I see your performance. Call it performance appraisal if you will. I don't think I can wait a year to let you know this, it would be unfair. After our meeting I'll probably make some informal notes on a blank sheet of paper and you're welcome to a copy of these. I'd also be interested, during this session, to learn what you think of my approach – although you've already given me a good indication – without filling in any forms! I always welcome such feedback." '

Giving instant feedback is a mark of the degree of openness, honesty, and trust that exists within any group of people. These values are at the cornerstone of any effective relationship, whether it be at work or at home. By being open and honest with each other, people have a chance to correct their mistakes, to re-examine their own behaviour, to challenge their own thinking, to develop their own values and views. In the absence of open and honest feedback, people close in on themselves and develop a distorted perception of their own effectiveness and abilities. The picture these people have of themselves tends to be highly sanitized. They cannot see the spots on their *own* face, all they do is see the spots on *other* people's faces. Such people are fearful of having a mirror held up to them. They are the type of people who insist that there are spots on the glass!

Giving instant feedback, therefore, is like using a mirror. You know when your hair is out of place or your hat is not straight. As a boss, you need to hold up a mirror to your people, and you need them to hold up a mirror to you.

PRINCIPLE:
Open, honest, and timely two-way communication.

PRACTICE:
Encourage your people to let you know what they think about what's going on and what you do.

As soon as possible, seize the opportunity to feed back to your people how you see their efforts.

Double-check what people say to you by giving them a summary of what you think they said.

14

Be tolerant (of mistakes)

To be successful, mistakes are essential.

Children learn to walk by falling over, learn to speak by saying the wrong words. The routes to success are littered with mistakes. Conversely, there is no route to success *without* mistakes.

One of the myths of modern management is that you can create the perfect model for the perfect implementation. Working parties will spend months thrashing out the best way of tackling a certain issue, attempting to distil their approach into a guideline or document for use throughout the organization. Invariably, the guideline is bland and meaningless. You cannot create a mistake-free model to resolve management issues.

Another myth is that people can learn and develop without making mistakes. There is an erroneous assumption that you can put people into a classroom to painlessly assimilate skills and knowledge that they can thereafter apply perfectly.

In traditional hierarchical organizations, people are frightened of making mistakes. They are like dogs with tails between their legs. They have been conditioned to believe that if a mistake is made, they will be punished. Their bosses, like aggressive hunters, seek out hapless victims who have screwed up, and, scenting blood, hound these people into submission.

Inevitably, it is always someone else who has made the mistake. The buck is passed. 'It's never me.'

Avoidance of making mistakes becomes a way of life in the

organization. But, it is equivalent to an avoidance of making decisions, an avoidance of taking action, an avoidance of initiative, an avoidance of speaking up, of asserting an opinion.

Progress is made by doing things badly to begin with, learning from the experience, and making improvements as a result. Without Orville and Wilbur Wright crashing their fragile 'Kitty Hawk' in the early 1900s we would not have the jumbo jet of today. Their longest flight lasted 59 seconds and covered 852 feet!

A mistake is a golden learning opportunity. Never deny yourself this in the university of life. Never cover up, never suppress the truth. Always admit your mistakes and learn from them. That is if you can see them. Many can't. That's why you need other people around you. They can help expose your mistakes, help you learn. It does require immense trust and a positive helping attitude towards each other. If you expose a mistake with the intention of punishing or hurting someone, you will fail. That person will clam up, become defensive, and attempt to deny the mistake.

The golden rule in handling mistakes is never aim to punish, but always aim to help. Most people accept that they are not perfect and want to learn how to improve, but not at the expense of having their mistakes, vulnerabilities, and inadequacies punished.

THE REAL SIN: 'NOT LEARNING FROM MISTAKES'

An American manager once gave me the following words of wisdom.

'My approach to mistakes is simple. My people are only allowed to make the *same* mistake twice. The third time they make the same mistake they are fired!

The first time I put it down to a lack of experience, a lack of training. But it's good that the person tried and failed. I expect the person to be honest and admit the mistake. We talk it through and agree how to prevent it happening again.

If the same mistake is made a second time, I get concerned. We have a more serious talk this time. I point out that we cannot continue to put the operation at risk if this type of mistake is repeated. So we agree further training and development.

The third time the mistake is made I fire the person.'

Having said all that, don't encourage your people to make mistakes! What you should do is encourage people to take risks, to speak up, to take initiatives, to take decisions. Essentially, you should be encouraging them to tolerate mistakes. Sometimes the rules are wrong and need revising. Then, it is the rule that is the mistake, not breaking it!

How you handle mistakes is a reflection of your own attitudes towards people, your own levels of understanding and sensitivity. The less you tolerate mistakes the less human you will appear to people. But there is a limit to that tolerance. Common sense dictates that you have to draw the line between damage of a minor or temporary nature and damage that can have catastrophic consequences: you allow a child to fall over in the safety of your living-room, but not by the side of a river. The trouble is that too many bosses see minor mistakes as catastrophes.

Most people don't *want* to make mistakes and are keen to learn from them to save any future embarrassment. Why tell them off when they have already learned? Look critically at yourself and eliminate any tendency to punish people (directly or indirectly) who fail. Discipline yourself to sit down with them and, in a friendly, positive manner, talk through how things can be done better next time. Mind you, if they continue to make the *same* mistakes, then you have another course of action to take (see the next section).

PRINCIPLE:
Mistakes are an essential part of learning.

PRACTICE:
Never punish a mistake; always learn from it.

15

Be intolerant (of bad behaviour)

Tolerating your people's bad behaviour is a reflection of your own inadequacies.

There is a limit to everything. Occasional, minor transgressions you can turn a blind eye to, but persistent transgressions reveal a deeper problem, on which you should act.

The borderline between what is acceptable and what is unacceptable is grey, confused, and will be subject to many interpretations. You cannot rule with a rod of iron, punishing every transgressor who puts a toe over the line. Conversely, you cannot allow people to get away with murder.

We are in the area of personal judgement here. You will have to make your own judgements about what behaviours you *can* tolerate and those you *can't*. The more your people behave badly in your presence, the greater is the probability that they will lack respect for you, are not motivated, and, in the end, will not achieve what is expected of them. As a boss, you can't allow this. From time to time, you are going to have to handle difficult situations involving bad behaviour. You won't find it easy, but it's not impossible.

When a person steps over the limit of what is acceptable to you (or what you are prepared to tolerate), it is imperative that you confront the bad behaviour immediately. In doing so, you should not cast aspersions, make value judgements, or assert negative motives of which you are suspicious. In other words, do not jump to conclusions. All you need to do is challenge the behaviour and ask for an explanation. Avoid making any value judgements until you have heard the person out.

BAD BEHAVIOUR

- Persistent lateness
- Jokes in bad taste (e.g., sexual, racist connotations, etc.)
- Excessive swearing
- Horseplay
- Negative body language (e.g., looking out of the window, sighing when in disagreement, shaking head in despair, etc.)
- Disrespectful attitudes towards others
- Putting people down (verbally)
- Not listening
- All types of bad manners (e.g., not saying 'Thank you', ignoring people, etc.)
- Talking behind someone's back
- Having a casual approach to work
- Poor appearance
- Untidiness
- Generally negative attitude (e.g., always complaining, it's always someone else's fault, etc.)
- Spending too much time on personal matters at work (e.g., too much chat, too many personal telephone calls, etc.)
- Abuse of trust (e.g., using the organization's supplies for personal reasons, etc.)
- Generally not bothering about anything
- Not taking care (e.g., on safety issues, leaving dangerous objects around, etc.)
- Not keeping promises (e.g., not delivering something on time, etc.)
- Covering up
- Telling half-truths or even lies
- Always knowing best, self-righteousness, arrogance
- Being patronizing

CONFRONTATIONS – OPENING MOVES

'I note you have been late on three occasions this week, I would be interested in your reasons for this.'

Taking a person aside after a meeting: 'When I was talking about the company's plans for this department I saw you sighing and going tut tut tut. I'm interested why you didn't speak up then. What was going on in your mind?'

'I am sure you will appreciate it if I am completely honest with you. Whenever we talk about making changes in your area, you always seem to find it all too difficult. It can never be done, for some reason that you say is outside your control. I am only expressing my personal view – I would be interested to learn how you see it.'

'Do you mind if I mention something personal? You came back from lunch yesterday smelling strongly of alcohol. I just wonder what your thoughts are on this and how you think other people might react, including me?'

Your people observe you every minute of the day. How you behave in handling other people's behaviour will have a tremendous influence on your own standing as a boss. If you are too rigid, not allowing minor transgressions, they will detest you. Conversely, if you are too lax, allowing certain individuals to fall below the standards of their mates, then they will see you as inept. Therefore, you need to establish very clearly in the minds of your people what you are prepared to accept and what you are not. You don't need to clarify what you will turn a blind eye to – they will find that out pretty quickly. Having clarified what's acceptable and what's not, it is very important that you are consistent and persistent in dealing with the unacceptable. Always confront it – never let people get away with the unacceptable.

Don't be afraid to talk these problems through with your people. Never personalize it, just ask what their views on lateness are, or swearing, or dirty jokes, or anything else you find unacceptable. Find out what they think and, if they find it objectionable, too, discuss with them the best way of handling the situation if someone steps out of line. In the end, you will find that everyone will converge on the types of behaviour that are acceptable to all, including you.

PRINCIPLE:
Bad behaviour will lead to poor work.

PRACTICE:
Always confront bad behaviour.

16

Take a genuine interest in everyone

People tend to do work well when you are interested in them, as people.

A great boss needs to relate to people on two levels. The first level is what interests people at work. The second level is what interests them outside work (the latter area is covered in a later section).

Most people spend a third of their day at work – longer if you take into account travelling time. Motivation drains away very quickly if a person's interest in their work is not sustained.

Without your active interest, your people will withdraw into themselves. They will develop relatively narrow perspectives of what their work is all about. The connection between what they do and what the organization (through you, the boss) wants of them will slowly erode. The danger is that without your active interest, their performance will deteriorate – they will begin to believe that you don't value them, don't appreciate them because you're not even aware of what they do.

Having said this, some people are difficult. They interpret too much interest as interference; these people *want* to be left alone to get on and do the job. Others welcome more interest. The skill of a great boss is to judge the level of interest they must take in what's happening to the people at work.

To achieve the right balance, it is critical that you question your own motives in taking an interest. Going through the motions or pretending to take an interest would be deceitful. People will detect an ulterior motive and assume you don't trust them or lack confidence in their ability. It is critical that you are *genuinely* interested in a person's well-being and *genuinely* want to help them if required. That help can be emotional support for a person who's feeling down because of a difficult situation, or it can be professional in helping resolve a technical problem, or it can simply be drawing on your own experience.

By taking an interest in your people, you will create a climate of mutual trust, of mutual understanding, and of mutual respect. You will be able to help them and they will be able to help you.

Sit alongside your people and take a real interest in what they're doing. Start talking about the sorts of problems they encounter. Find out what they really enjoy about their job, what they dislike about it. Explore the various working relationships they have in the office or factory, who they talk to, who they go to lunch with, who phones

---

AREAS OF INTEREST

- **Problems encountered**
- **Resolution of problems**
- **Initiatives taken**
- **Overall progress**
- **Unexpected events**
- **Relations with other departments/sections**
- **What's happening in the organization**
- **What's happening in the market-place**
- **Organizational changes**
- **Changes affecting a person's work**
- **New equipment coming in**
- **Future plans**
- **Relations with customers**
- **Relations with suppliers**
- **Relations with other people who work for you**

51

them up, who writes them memos or letters. Find out what they think about how other departments and sections operate. Try to discover the things they feel constrain them as well as the things that really help them.

Also, take an interest in their personal welfare and their careers. Find out whether or not they are encountering any problems, for example with their working conditions or the equipment they use, or with operating manuals, or with other departments. Find out what their ambitions are and whether they see themselves developing further over the coming years.

By taking a genuine interest in your people, you will obviously learn much about them and be in a much better position to come to sensible decisions when changes need to be made.

It is also important that you create in your people an interest in what is going on outside the immediate boundaries of their workplace. You can do this by exposing them to the operations of other departments and sections, by encouraging them to get to know as many people in the organization as possible. You can also do it by training, as well as by encouraging your people to meet customers and suppliers. Travel provides another opportunity for such expansion of knowledge. You can also create interest by demonstrating how your people's contributions add value to the organization. By broadening their horizons, you will be generating opportunities to relate more effectively to your people and also enabling them to work effectively. Most people do much better if they can relate their work to the progress being made in general by the organization.

So, take a walk, and show a real interest in what's going on. It will pay dividends.

PRINCIPLE:
People respond positively to bosses who take an interest in them.

PRACTICE:
Create as many opportunities as possible to show that interest.

17

Express yourself (your opinions, your personality)

Never be a clone of the system.

Almost 40 years ago, William H. Whyte published an influential work entitled *The Organization Man* (Simon & Schuster, 1956), in which he explored the issue of conformity within large organizations. To quote: 'The organization man is imprisoned in brotherhood. Because his area of manoeuvre seems so small and because the trapping so mundane, his fight lacks the heroic cast'.

The issue of conformity poses an important dilemma for any boss. Consistent conformance effectively subordinates the 'true self' to the dictates of the organization. Conversely, failure to conform risks rejection by the very organization on which you are dependent.

As always, there is a balance. No organization can operate successfully without subscribing to a shared set of values, beliefs and goals. However, those values and beliefs should not be so constrained in definition as to severely limit individuals initiating their own pursuit of the goals they are paid to achieve. Nor should these values and beliefs be so rigid in application that they cannot be challenged and developed.

More explicitly, no organization should tell you how to think, how to behave, and how to act. Its values and beliefs should be geared to *what* it has to achieve rather than *how* to achieve it.

Put another way, organizations can only survive and succeed if the individuals within them are allowed to be themselves. You must be your own person. You would not be there if you did not want to contribute to the overall achievement of the organization's goals, but to make that contribution you will need a fair degree of freedom of manoeuvre to express yourself, be yourself, and do what you believe is right to achieve what you are paid to achieve.

If you are not yourself, if you attempt to simulate the type of behaviour you interpret the organization requires of you, then you will fail. People will not be able to relate to you, they will be unsure of you, they will not know what to make of you. They will see you as an organization man (or woman). They might as well just read the policy as refer to you.

To be successful, therefore, you should not be looking to the organization for guidance on how to behave, on what to say, on what to do. You should be looking to yourself.

When you are with your people, it *is you* that should be coming across, not some paraphrasing of the organization's position on this, that, or the other. Your people should be able to see the colour of your personality, the strengths of your opinions, and the weight of your own personal commitments and beliefs. Too many managers are 'grey' – suppressing their true self, failing to assert their views. They fear non-compliance and end up being nothing. They become conditioned by the organization and, thus, become mediocre.

People love bosses who ooze personality, who are vibrant and energetic. Such energy comes from within. It comes from a high degree of personal drive based on strongly held convictions and beliefs, and a genuine ambition to meet major challenges and achieve outstanding success.

To be successful as a boss, you have to look at yourself, then look at how you put yourself across. Do not fear what the organization thinks, that senior executives might disagree with you or dislike the opinions you express. But, be open to persuasion in the same way that you would like others to be persuaded by you. Have the debate and be prepared to change as your beliefs develop and you learn how to apply them more effectively.

Seek advice from people you trust and behave accordingly, but do not trust the policy manuals to guide your behaviour. What these manuals ask you to do will either be common sense or unnecessary. If it's common sense do it, if it's unnecessary don't!

In expressing your opinions, take care to be constructive. If you tell your people your own boss is crazy you will fail. If that really *is* your opinion, you should be confronting your boss with it, no one else. Opinions that divide are damaging and should be suppressed. They are unnecessary. In expressing yourself, attempt always to be positive and constructive. By all means express an opinion that 'The new TQM system is rubbish', but always back it up with an opinion on how quality should be improved. In expressing your view about the new TQM system, avoid having a go at the person who put it in. Avoid being personal.

Your opinions should be geared to achieving your goals. Your goals should never be to damage other people or the organization as a whole.

PRINCIPLE:
Be yourself, but be positive.

PRACTICE:
Look within yourself. Express yourself freely, but never with the intention of damaging other people or the organization.

Ensure that your people know what you stand for personally.

18

Value your people and their efforts

A sense of being valued is one of the most important motivating factors for people at work.

Perhaps the biggest and most frequent moan I ever hear when running seminars is that people don't feel that their efforts are really valued. Despite all the attempts at sophisticated performance appraisal systems, it seems that some bosses' perceptions of their people's efforts are totally divorced from those of the people themselves.

Some bosses are so busy doing other things they are totally unaware of the hard work their people are putting in, the problems they are facing, and how they are tackling them. These bosses seem to have no idea of what's going on. Furthermore, these bosses are totally unaware of the extensive talents their people have. The end result is that people feel devalued. Their skills, knowledge, and experience are not used to the full, and what efforts they do put in generally go unnoticed.

It's even worse when appraisal time comes round and these bosses have to concoct answers to complete the review forms. You might think I'm exaggerating, but this problem really is endemic. Many people just don't know where they stand with their bosses.

If there is any art to motivation, then it is all about making people feel valued. Pay is one simple measure, but it is not enough in itself. People need to receive genuine appreciation for a job done well; they need to feel that their contribution has been recognized and valued. Some people have greater needs in this respect than others – some need constant reassurance while others find frequent expressions of appreciation embarrassing.

There are two obvious steps in this process. First, you have to clearly identify and recognize the efforts of your people. Second, you have to demonstrate that you value these efforts.

In recognizing effort, you will have to differentiate between the routine and the exceptional. Many people routinely work exceptionally hard, regularly dealing with difficult situations – irate customers, complicated problems, uncooperative colleagues, and so on. These routine efforts need to be recognized and valued accordingly. On less frequent occasions, people will make an exceptional effort: perhaps delivering an urgent order for a customer, or tackling a crisis, or implementing a major change. The way you recognize and value these exceptions could well be different to that given for the routine contribution.

The process of recognizing and valuing your people's efforts, therefore, is one of your major priorities. It is questionable whether the use of bureaucratic methods, such as performance appraisal, is of any help with this. Expressing appreciation, surely, is a matter of common sense. The key is to find the most appropriate way of doing so. Giving a rating of eight out of ten and a small performance-related pay increase to go with it is rarely appropriate.

Managing people is an art, and there are a thousand different ways in which you can value your people's efforts. Your people really do need to be convinced that you appreciate them. To do this you need to exercise all your creative and innovative energies.

Words are fine, if you are totally sincere, but words can be limited. The repetition of the same old phrases about what a great job they are doing devalues the currency. So, you have to invent new ways of showing how you value your people's efforts. Sending them to top hotels to attend training seminars is one way. Sending a card with a note of appreciation is another. A bunch of flowers, a bottle of whisky, a simple letter … there are a thousand ways. You have to choose.

As a matter of routine you will need to get the pay right, and it goes without saying that pay is a fundamental expression of value, but, once into the job, people will need to have their day-by-day efforts valued. If they exceed the monthly target, then, perhaps, a celebration is called for, to show how much you value their success.

Showing how you value your people and their efforts is so critical. Neglecting to do so effectively devalues your people. There is no middle road. Even giving people time values them. Sharing confidences values them. Speaking to them as equals values them. Listening to people values them. Once people sense you value them, they will extend their efforts for you, and there will be more to value. It becomes a reinforcing process. The converse is also true. The more you complain and criticize, the more you devalue. Criticism should be aimed at helping people you really value to increase their worth in your eyes – that's constructive criticism.

If you have reservations about your people, concerns about their lack of effort, then you must tackle the problem head on. Too many bosses send out indirect signals for people to read into. These are frequently misinterpreted and, as a result, people are totally confused about where they stand in their boss's eyes. In other words, they are not sure whether they are valued or not. Varying perceptions of people's efforts cause immense dissension at work. To succeed as a boss, you must really believe in your people. That belief must be reflected in an open, honest, and trusting relationship with them, which is of such a kind that they feel valued when you help them overcome the inadequacies that concern you.

PRINCIPLE:
To work effectively, people need to feel valued.

PRACTICE:
Identify what you really value about your people. Spell it out to them.

Look out for exceptional effort and find creative new ways of demonstrating that you really value such effort.

19

Get your people to sell

The reason many companies fail is that they miss a thousand opportunities to sell.

It really does puzzle me why so few people try to sell me things. We have planted a myth in our minds that the only people who should sell are salespeople. What nonsense! Of course the salespeople see this as their role, are protective of it, and resent other people intruding on their territory. They will make out that there is some special skill in selling, but there isn't.

Selling is all about having a product or service you believe will be of value to your customers (or potential customers). It really is a matter of belief. That belief should be shared by every single person in the organization.

The second myth about selling is that only salespeople are exposed to selling opportunities. There is no doubt that they do have prime responsibility to create these opportunities and capitalize upon them. However, most other employees have opportunities, too. For example, it surprises me how often receptionists in hotels do no more than check me in, or waiters in restaurants do no more than take my order, or assistants in shoe shops do no more than sell me the shoes I saw in the window. It surprises me how infrequently front-line staff strike up conversations with customers, just in case they can discover something more the customer wants. Great bosses help their people convert from being ordertakers to all-round salespeople. The opportunities are boundless.

It should be mandatory teaching in every organization that every interface with a customer is a selling opportunity, whether this be directly or indirectly.

Staff who are enthusiastic indirectly sell their organization and its products and services while those who are indifferent and unenthusiastic frequently inhibit customers from buying.

How rare it is to go into a book shop where the assistant says, 'If you like this type of book I can recommend another one which will be just up your street ...' Tempting, eh? This happened to me recently when buying a CD. The assistant went out of his way to chat to me and then said, 'This album you're buying is really great. Have you heard the group's previous release? I'd really recommend that, too'. So I bought that as well. I went to buy one and came out with two (and both were excellent).

Every employee must identify with the organization's end product. They must be proud to be associated with it.

The great bosses ensure that this happens and put a lot of effort into maximizing their people's exposure to the product, so they have first-hand experience of it, value it, believe in it.

If this can be achieved, then employees will convince a lot of people they come into contact with that the product is worth having. The beauty of this is that it gives an added dimension to each person's job. Most people love to push their company's products.

Product awareness and product training for all employees thus become essential activities in the operation of any successful organization.

As the boss, you will need to initiate this product awareness and enthusiasm. If you produce food, let your people eat it. If you are in the travel business, encourage your people to travel. If you are in financial services, let them benefit from some of the products. If you are in manufacturing, get the salespeople to practise by selling to your people. If you are in retail, persuade your people that for every sale to a customer, there is an opportunity to make a second. If you are in the hotel business, get your people to sell additional services – dinner reservations when guests check in, after-dinner drinks when ordering desserts. If you are in hairdressing, make sure you book your customer's next appointment in six weeks' time. If you are in banking, find out when your customers are going on holiday, then make the arrangements for their traveller's cheques.

Selling means being one step ahead of your customers. If you are one step *behind*, the risk is they will go elsewhere for what you could be supplying. Selling means having very sensitive antennae about your customers' needs. Selling means being the first there to meet your customers' requirements, saving them the trouble of going elsewhere.

Salespeople don't have sole rights on being sensitive to customer needs and meeting their requirements. That should be the province of everyone who is in contact with a customer or potential customer.

Take photocopies of these three pages as a basis for a discussion with your people and identify further opportunities to sell the excellent products and services your organization supplies. You'll be amazed at the success that results.

PRINCIPLE:
Every employee should seize opportunities to sell the organization's products and services.

PRACTICE:
Sit down with your people and brainstorm out as many ideas as possible for selling your products and services.

Then, implement these ideas.

20

Show courage

Difficult problems rarely go away. The best bosses have the courage to face up to them.

It is critical that you show courage as a boss. On major decisions this sometimes means standing on principle and even putting your job on the line (this is dealt with in a later section).

But, courage is also required in dealing with a whole array of difficult situations that inevitably crop up in your everyday work.

The worst bosses tend to shy away from difficult situations – they stick their head in the sand, pretend that it is not happening. They go around avoiding difficult people and difficult situations. They duck difficult decisions.

These are people who will not face up to the truth about themselves, will not examine, nor address, their own vulnerabilities and inadequacies. They seem to be at a loss as to how to handle difficult situations.

There are other people who, talented and intelligent as they are, never say anything. They keep quiet, rarely speaking at meetings, rarely pushing their views forwards. It is almost as if they are frightened of being shown up. Again, it is to do with vulnerabilities.

We are all vulnerable, but, in this tough old world, the most successful people learn to ride it out. They develop the courage to put their views forward, to take the risk of making decisions, and, therefore, making mistakes. They learn how to handle difficult people and difficult situations.

To develop this courage, you must always start by looking at yourself and face up to your own vulnerabilities. It is too easy to assume that a problem is beyond you, is outside your control, is the fault of another, is too difficult or even impossible to resolve. Sometimes that problem is no more than allowing other people to force their will on you because they seem to know more than you and like to give the impression of being right all the time.

There is no textbook way to develop courage, other than jumping in the deep end and demonstrating it when required (you cannot learn to swim simply by reading a book). It means speaking out. It means taking risks. It means trying.

To develop courage, therefore, you need to be aware of any tendency to shy away from difficult issues. Common sense will tell you that normally the problem will not go away by avoiding it. Question yourself as to *why* you are shying away, try to identify the reasons for this. It might well be that you are not sure whether you

---

DIFFICULT SITUATIONS REQUIRING COURAGE

- **Dealing with someone who is always putting you down**

- **Handling bad behaviour**

- **Making a decision on how best to reduce staff levels**

- **Pursuing a promise you rashly made to somebody but that you are subsequently unsure about**

- **Admitting your own mistakes and failings**

- **Helping cynical people become more positive**

- **Doing something you don't like**

- **Taking big risks**

- **Speaking up at meetings when everyone else seems to know more than you**

- **Expressing your concerns to other people when you know they are going to react adversely to what you say**

- **Responding to somebody who asks you to do something against your principles**

- **Taking an honest look at yourself as other people see you, with the risk that you might not like what you see. And, subsequently, having the courage to do something about it**

---

are right or wrong and are fearful of being exposed if you confront the issue. It might be that you lack confidence in handling any adverse reaction. Think through the issue and try to identify the most sensible course of action. Examine this course from different angles. Dive deeper than your initial emotional response (of avoidance) and try to work through the best course of action in your own mind.

Working through this process will help you reinforce your own basic beliefs, beliefs you know are shared by most people. This will give you courage and the ability to show it by confronting the situation.

As an excellent boss, you will also want to create a climate among your people in which they have the courage to speak out and make difficult decisions. It is a matter of giving people confidence by listening to them carefully, respecting them, and valuing what they say and do. This will reinforce their own reserves of courage, as well as your own!

PRINCIPLE:
Handling difficult situations requires courage.

PRACTICE:
Try to identify those issues that you lack the courage to address, and think through why. Then, address the issue.

Create an atmosphere among your people where they have the courage to speak up and talk about difficult situations and to do difficult things.

21

Be positive

A positive result requires a positive mind.

There is a cliché about the half empty jug which is of particular relevance to anyone striving to manage properly. It is not only how you see life but also how you see the situation at work. Threats, shortfalls, deficiencies, failures, and other people's perceived inadequacies are, in fact, opportunities.

Cynicism is rife today. Sometimes I think we British people are the world's leading experts in stating problems. There is nothing more we enjoy than a good moan and groan. We delight in pontificating about people's incompetence, forever amazed by decisions made by politicians, senior executives, and others. It would all be so easy if they took our advice, if they did things the way we think they should. We acquire five seconds' knowledge on a subject and become experts who know better than people who have studied the subject their whole lives.

Such cynicism does have its positive attributes, in that nothing can be taken for granted, that everything is questioned and challenged, that people have to account for their decisions. There is no harm in being subjected to scrutiny by highly critical people – it can force out the best in us.

Equally, there can be something sinister about people who are continually positive. They can come across as being false. It's almost as if they have an instinctive reflex action of being positive whatever the situation, saying 'Yes, that's great!' when you know full well it is far from being so.

It is a question of the superficial versus the deep-rooted belief. A great boss will seek out the positive aspect of any situation, will look for the positive attributes in any person. When in doubt, a great boss will take positive action as opposed to negative. That does not mean to say that negative aspects and negative attributes are neglected. To do so would be at the organization's peril. The positive approach is to identify the negative and convert it into the positive. It is to recognize the half empty jug and fill it rather than eulogize about how great the half *full* jug is. It is to be honest about Bill's limitations at making presentations rather than kid him along and say 'That was a fantastic presentation' when, in fact, it was terrible.

There is a secret to all this. It is to refrain from making value judgements. Being positive is not about setting yourself up as God to be the supreme judge of all others' behaviour, actions, and decisions. It is about moving forward, making progress, achieving results, seeking improvement, and, overall, making something very beneficial happen. Being negative is all about inflicting damage, either deliberately or inadvertently. It is about lowering morale, hindering progress, resisting change, bad-mouthing others' valiant efforts, rubbishing success.

Having a good moan and groan can have extremely positive results. It can be a cathartic experience, it can be like a therapy, but it should never damage others. Having a good moan and groan should always be aimed at bringing about positive actions to redress the problems. And that's where you as a boss come in. Don't discourage people from opening up and expressing themselves, no matter how bad they feel. Instead, encourage them to take an objective view as to how issues can be constructively addressed.

There is another cliché about never hanging out your dirty linen in public. That doesn't mean to say you shouldn't *have* dirty linen, nor wash it and air it, but take care when airing problems – and always find the right forum. It is right to develop open, honest, and trusting relationships with your customers, but don't abuse such trust by confiding in them about the immense problems you have, for example, with your director. Talking behind someone's back is being negative. The positive approach is to address the person with whom you have the problem, in this case your director.

Therefore, avoid running people or your organization or its products down all the time. Identify problems, yes, but address them in a positive way.

BE POSITIVE

About:

- your company's products and services
- the people who work with you
- your own boss
- your company
- your competitors
- your customers
- your suppliers
- the opportunities facing you all
- changes taking place
- new initiatives
- feedback about the way you go about things and your overall contribution
- other people's ideas
- mistakes (learning from them)
- failure (using it as a springboard for success)
- yourself as a person

PRINCIPLE:
The pursuit of progress by being positive.
The danger of negative thoughts, words, and actions.

PRACTICE:
Only state a problem you can address and do something about.
Ignore problems you can do nothing about.

22

Get around (take note and take notes)

To be a great boss you need sensitive antennae.

Whenever possible, it is best to get the information first-hand, especially when it comes to what people are thinking. Second-hand information about what's in people's minds gets distorted, or diluted, or filtered. The impact is lost when it is put on to a piece of paper or comes to you in the form of a verbal report from an intermediary.

Don't be frightened to dip right down into the organization, even if there are intermediate managers and supervisors who might resent you 'interfering' with their people. They shouldn't. In fact, they should welcome you looking at their patch as you will be able to see things they can't – after all, 'two heads are better than one'.

When I was a director of a large organization I used to find two types of reactions from managers to my wandering around to get a feel for what was going on. As a matter of courtesy I would always inform a manager or supervisor that I'd like to spend half an hour or so having a look around and meeting some of his or her people. The first category of managers always welcomed it. These types had no fear of what their people might say to me. As far as they were concerned, everything should be out on the table, there should be no secrets at any level. The second category of managers would always be apprehensive about a senior executive wandering around and, more often than not, would insist on accompanying me. These types would treat it like a royal visit, politely introducing their people to me and 'giving them the eye' to ensure that nothing untoward was ever said.

You don't have to be a senior executive or director to get around your patch. In fact, the more you get around and get to know what's going on – in the plant, offices, and in people's minds – the less you have to fear when a senior person descends on your territory for an informal walk around.

While your walk arounds should always be informal and relatively casual, never treat them as a low-priority activity. In fact, they should be your top priority. Refuse to cram your diary so full of meetings that you don't have time for this vital aspect of your work. Discipline yourself to keep plenty of blank space in your diary (an hour or two a day should be adequate).

When you are responsible for more than one location, the logistics get a little more difficult, but not impossible. Schedule regular walk arounds for each location.

Get people to talk about themselves when you go around, not just about work, but about other things as well. People are not going to open up to you first time, but if they see you regularly and get to know you, their trust will grow and they will be more likely to reveal what's really happening, especially if you take a genuine interest in what they are doing and the problems they are encountering. It's all about developing and improving relationships.

Inevitably people will raise problems with you and, as a boss, they will expect you to fix them. It is critical, therefore, that you take notes of points raised and that you take action afterwards.

INACTION AFTER A PROMISE OF ACTION

'I had this appraisal nine months ago and my boss promised me some supervisory training. I felt this would help with my promotion prospects. I've heard nothing since then. Nor do I see my boss much. He did come around about a month ago and I asked him about the training he promised. He grunted and said nothing. It went in one ear and out the other. I know he'll forget and do nothing about it.'

Too many bosses go through the motions of getting around, fail to take note of what is said to them, and, therefore, fail to take action. The points people raise might not be important to you, but they are important to them. So, jot down what they say and be meticulous in following up any issue raised. Even if you can't resolve their problems, you are duty bound to go back to tell them why you can't. Whatever people say to you should be treated seriously, even if you consider the point to be minor.

ALWAYS AVAILABLE

'Our previous Managing Director was the best boss I ever had. He was always available no matter how busy he was. Every morning he would spend at least an hour walking round the offices and the factory. You could rely on him popping in to see you first thing to enquire how things were going. It was a golden opportunity for me to raise any issue with him and for him to update me on what had been happening. I never abused his time, it was rare that we had more than five minutes together on these occasions.

Additionally he would have regular monthly individual meetings with me as well as team meetings. Furthermore he was always prepared to see me if I wanted, finding time to fit me in no matter how hectic his schedule was.'

Getting around is one of the most basic tasks for any boss. But what you do afterwards with the information is critical.

PRINCIPLE:
Developing trust, being sensitive to people's needs, good informal communications, listening and taking action.

PRACTICE:
Discipline yourself to get around frequently.

Always take notes of what people say to you.

Always follow up with action and report back.

23

Meet your customers

Out of sight, out of mind.

Meeting your customers face to face brings everything into perspective. You begin to see things in a different light. You eliminate any tendency to take them for granted. You remember that you wouldn't be there if it wasn't for them.

Hopefully your people will already be in frequent contact with your customers, whether they be internal or external, but that is no excuse for you not to get out and see them yourselves.

You cannot manage any business, even if it is an internal business unit, by just reading customer service analyses prepared by your people, or listening to their presentations. When it comes to customer service, second-hand reporting *must* be supplemented by first-hand experience with customers. Face-to-face contact brings your people's reports to life, brings the customer view into focus.

Furthermore, it reinforces (in the minds of your people) the value you place on getting the vital customer service aspect of your business right.

Gone are the days when few people had direct contact with customers. In this day and age everyone has customers, and the better you know them the better it is. This is the era of the inverted triangle when everyone within any organization, large or small, has to point towards customers. A failure on a boss' part to do so will inevitably lead to failure on his people's part, too. There will, consequently, be a failure of that manager's business.

MEETING YOUR CUSTOMERS

A ten-point action chart for both *internal* and *external* customers

1 Arrange to go to see your customers for an informal chat
2 Fix a formal meeting to review the service provided
3 Drop in to see your customers
4 Keep in touch by telephone – 'How are things going?'
5 Carry out surveys – 'Tell us what you think of us'
6 Implement research programmes – 'Help us develop our service'
7 Invite your customers to come and see your operation – 'Meet the team'
8 Write and inform your customers – 'We are making these improvements and changes'
9 Get customers to participate in your training activities
10 Introduce customers to your boss

Bosses who place emphasis on meeting customers send a signal to their people that the customer is all-important. Furthermore, whatever is discussed through these customer contacts can provide a useful focus for team discussions. It can be the source of developmental activity and improvement actions.

The ways in which bosses behave towards customers reflects their own attitudes and prejudices. Bosses who passionately feel that customers are the be-all and end-all of their jobs reflect this in the way they go about their everyday business. Anything to do with a customer becomes a source of excitement. This fascination inevitably extends into the team and will be reflected in the way they approach their work.

The differences in attitudes towards customers can often be marked (you only have to look at your own experiences outside work). It is all a matter of wanting to please customers, of wanting to put yourself out for them, of making them feel important because you genuinely feel they are important. That attitude spreads. A mechanistic approach to meeting customers will achieve nothing unless you (and your people) are passionately interested in them.

The worst thing you can do is pay lip-service to the importance of customers. Regrettably, too many bosses do this. Having a genuine appreciation of the importance of customers and a genuine desire to learn more about them as well as help them is essential if a boss is to be really successful.

PRINCIPLE:
Customers are the reason for the existence of the business, the boss, and his or her people.

A genuine belief that customers are all-important in your line of business.

Get to know your customers as well as you can.

PRACTICE:
Seize every possible opportunity to meet your customers.

Challenge your own attitudes towards your customer. Are they sufficiently positive?

24

Allow your people to develop

You cannot develop people – they develop themselves.

All you can do is provide your people with a wide range of opportunities to develop and encourage them to seize them. Examples are shown on the opposite page.

The indirect result of encouraging your people to develop is that the business will develop, too. Such learning motivates, and your customers will benefit from the energy and excitement generated by those eager to improve their skills and extend their knowledge. People are as good as dead when they stop learning, and there are many like that around in large organizations – and the customers know it.

As a great boss, therefore, you must devote an inordinate amount of time energy and resources to seeking out and providing development opportunities for your people. It is a never-ending search, but the opportunities are endless.

One of the first things I was taught at Mars when I was a Production Manager in the late 1960s was that the best bosses get their people promoted out of their section or department. The worst bosses cling on to people, claiming that they are indispensable, fearing that letting them go will damage the operation. The best bosses take pride in seeing their people develop and move on to greater challenges elsewhere, whether it be within the organization or outside. In fact, the best bosses are forever encouraging their people to take on new responsibilities, to extend themselves.

DEVELOPMENT OPPORTUNITIES

- Regular job swaps
- Honest feedback
- Travel
- Increased responsibility
- Accountability for key projects
- Doing the boss' jobs
- Visiting progressive organizations
- Meeting progressive people
- Studying how we do it, and doing it better
- Reading stimulating books
- Formal study (college, etc.)
- Seminars, workshops
- Learning from experience (self-questioning)
- Coaching and personal tuition
- Counselling
- Meaningful training
- Inspiration
- Self-extension (setting even tougher targets for oneself)
- Moving jobs
- Exposure to new thinking
- Writing books, reports (focuses the mind)
- Giving presentations (you have to know what you're talking about)
- Encouraging a passionate desire to learn and develop

There is a myth around that training and development can be left to centralized personnel and training departments who eke out control by grabbing training budgets and pretending to pioneer progressive techniques for improving the organization. If these people have any role at all it is to provide a reservoir of training and development opportunities for people throughout the organization to seize. The training budgets should be pushed down to the lowest possible level. Those who are accountable for achieving the results should have the budgets to ensure that they can secure development opportunities to maximize their chances of achieving those results. The role of the centre is to facilitate, to consult, to act as a procurer, if not provider, of the effective training required by line managers. It is definitely not to control training and development activities.

Your challenge today is to sit down and reflect on what conscious efforts you have made over the last three months to provide your people with opportunities to develop. In fact, if you really are a great boss, your people will have come knocking at your door to get your support for opportunities they want to grasp. On reflection, if you are truly a great boss you won't have a door and they will have involved you in making their decision!

Most great bosses I know get a terrific buzz out of seeing their people develop. They get excited by their progress. The process of learning can be an underrated activity. It should not stop after school or university.

Sit down with your team and ask a simple question: 'What have we all learned over the last three months? How have we developed? What are the lessons for the future? What have we learned about ourselves?'

One of the things I do is keep a diary. It gives me an opportunity to reflect on the day, to learn the lessons, and identify ways of doing it better next time. Why not use some similar device to review your own experiences and focus on improvements?

Learning should be essential throughout life, and the opportunities are there to do so every day! Development is the process of seizing these daily opportunities. The business will benefit accordingly.

PRINCIPLES:
To develop your business you must allow your people to develop.

PRACTICE:
Sit down with each person you work with and review what development opportunities they have taken advantage of in recent times.

Agree on future opportunities, ensure that facilities are available for them to take advantage of and encourage each person to seize them.

25

Relax

To release your full potential, relax!

Management is full of myths. One of them is that to succeed you have to work exceptionally long hours and create an impression that you are forever under pressure and therefore very busy. A virtue is made out of stress, of scurrying around, stepping in and out of aeroplanes and trains, of having impossible bosses, of lurching from one crisis to another.

Relax!

We're back to common sense again and what you know for a fact. The fact is that you cannot work effectively unless you relax regularly. This means relaxing at work, relaxing when away on business, relaxing at home.

Unless you relax your people will not be able to do so. They will sense your tension, will be apprehensive of you, fearing you might snap.

The amazing thing about relaxation is that it clears the mind. You begin to see things differently. Pressures suddenly disappear, things come into perspective. Furthermore, you get new ideas. A solution to a major problem will occur to you.

To be creative you need stimuli. You will not find stimuli when you are rushing around trying to catch up with everything. Relaxation brings that stimuli. Suddenly you will be bubbling with new ideas, new energy, and a fresh motivation to crack what yesterday seemed to be an intractable problem.

None of this is new. In fact, it is perfectly obvious to most of us. Yet, the paradox is that too few bosses put it into practice. Perhaps there

---

TEN RULES FOR RELAXATION

1 Always take time off for lunch, go for a walk (or swim if there's a pool nearby) and eat lightly afterwards
2 Do not drink alcohol during working hours, it will not relax you
3 Make some tea for your people towards the end of the day, put your feet up, and chew the cud with them
4 Do not work late more than two nights a week. Make sure you get home *before* the kids go to bed at least three nights a week
5 Never take more than three hours' work home at the weekend. Always devote one whole day at the weekend to enjoying non-work activities
6 When travelling, don't work all the time – spend at least 50 per cent of the journey time reading a book, magazine or whatever that has nothing to do with work
7 Do not feel compelled to be doing something all the time. If you find you have five minutes spare between meetings, do nothing! Just sit back in your chair and relax
8 Walk everywhere. Upstairs, downstairs, to the station, to town.
9 Never leave things to the last minute. Always take an earlier train than you need and relax when you get to the other end
10 Always take your holidays

---

is a deep psychological reason for people liking to be driven by events, as opposed to driving themselves. Managers who rush around from one crisis to another are certainly driven by events. Others rise above it, take everything in their stride, never seem to panic, always seem to find time to put their feet up. They see things differently. They have control. When you are relaxed, you are more able to take control. When you are too highly stressed, the danger is that you begin to lose control, you lose perspective, you get into continual reactionary mode.

Inevitably, there is a balance and I am not advocating a continual state of relaxation. The key is to create opportunities every day to relax, to find breathing space, to recharge your batteries. It can be five minutes here or three weeks in the Mediterranean on holiday.

If you want to take a more philosophical view, ask yourself what life is all about. Isn't it to occasionally enjoy yourself, to do what you want? We live in a very hostile world when one moment you're in a job and the next minute you're not, through no fault of your own.

I've seen too many people rushing around, giving every available minute of the day to their employer, only to be made redundant because of the latest recession. I've seen people destroy their family relationships by giving everything to their company. What for? Does anyone appreciate you more for working excessive hours.

As soon as you relax not only will your people relax, but your family will, too. It doesn't require money to relax. It just requires a reordering of your priorities and finding a bit of time for yourself and everyone else.

PRINCIPLE:
Without relaxation, people become less effective.

PRACTICE:
Discipline yourself to stop working at regular intervals and relax by doing something enjoyable.

26

Give people their heads

In a traditional, hierarchical organization only 5 per cent of a person's head is used for purposes of work.

There is a well known fact that many managers ignore. This is that most people are much more capable than they seem, especially at work.

It is a salutary exercise to sit down with people and find out what they do when they're not at work. Unfettered by the constraints of the organization, most people use their heads effectively, not only to survive with limited resources, but to undertake a range of positive and satisfying tasks. Most even manage their own money quite well (and I'm not talking about peanuts here), even if it is a struggle occasionally. They make decisions that can cost them tens of thousands, and occasionally hundreds of thousands of pounds. They organize and manage families, frequently juggling ten conflicting activities at any one time. They are exceptionally creative. Some write books, others play great music, or excel at sport, or take pride in tending beautiful gardens, or devote their lives to worthwhile social causes, or undertake the most complex DIY tasks to enhance their homes. Others seek to improve themselves through home study and the pursuit of additional qualifications. The exciting activities people pursue outside the workplace are endless.

What is well known and frequently neglected is that very little of this energy, creativity, and intellect is transferred to the workplace, especially if it is run in a traditional, hierarchical way.

The potential that you can release, as a great boss, is enormous. You can recognize and harness this latent talent and put it to use in a way that benefits both the employee and the organization.

By giving people their head you indicate that you really trust and

---

YOU MUST LET PEOPLE

- Organize their own schedules (rosters, holidays, working hours, etc.)
- Organize their own working arrangements (who does what, when, and where)
- Set up their own training within budgets agreed with you
- Pursue interesting new ideas
- Have some budget to experiment with, to make improvements
- Have their say on whatever they like
- Challenge you on anything you do that affects their work
- Celebrate success
- Decide on their own office/work environment (colour schemes, where to put the plants, etc.)
- Choose what they can wear at work (providing it doesn't infringe health and safety requirements, and providing it doesn't infringe the overall corporate identity)
- Take the lead role in monitoring and reviewing their own performance
- Take initiatives without consulting you
- Make mistakes
- Change senseless rules (which they would otherwise break)
- Decide on their own travel arrangements
- Speak freely to whoever they like, including the press (but providing no confidential information is disclosed)
- Decide on how best to handle poor performers and others who abuse the system

---

value them. The more freedoms you give them the more likely they are to be successful. When trusted, most people are honest enough to admit that they don't have the skills and knowledge to undertake certain tasks. That is where you come in as the boss. Your role becomes one of adviser, assistant, supporter, trainer, coach, guide, consultant, reviewer, communicator, listener, sounding board, motivator. You become a source of encouragement to the group. Your role is to generate enthusiasm, to lift people up when they are down, to quieten them down when they are too high, to offer wise words, to give balance, to reinforce the overall direction for the organization and, therefore, the framework within which they must work.

In giving people their heads it is important to differentiate between *what* people are seeking to achieve and *how* they achieve it.

The directors of commercial companies are accountable to shareholders for *what* they achieve. Similarly, senior executives in public service organizations are accountable to politicians for *what* they achieve in relation to policy implementation.

Giving people their heads is all about allowing people freedom to decide how best to achieve what you require of them in pursuit of the organization's goals. Inevitably you cannot totally divorce the 'what' from the 'how'. Your people will, to a degree, have to be involved in deciding what has to be achieved, although, ultimately, you, as boss, will be accountable for this. You cannot arbitrarily decide on the 'whats' without due consideration of the 'hows'.

The worst thing you can do as a boss is interfere in how your people are going about their jobs. Having clarified what they are there for, just let them get on and do it!

PRINCIPLE:
The best results are achieved when people are trusted to decide on how best to go about their work.

PRACTICE:
As a boss, concentrate on clarifying what has to be achieved, and what has been achieved. Then provide support to your people in how they go about achieving what you require of them.

27

Be courteous

Courtesy is the hallmark of a civilized approach.

I might be old-fashioned but sometimes I get the distinct impression that people today are becoming less and less courteous. On two occasions recently I have taken people out to lunch. On neither occasion did either have the courtesy to write me a follow-up 'Thank you' letter. I say to myself, 'Am I being too sensitive?' Should I really mind if I write to someone and don't get a reply, or someone doesn't ring back?

My problem is this. Many executives devote an inordinate amount of time trying to improve quality standards for their products and services, yet their own personal behaviours are frequently lamentably discourteous (for excellent examples of discourteous behaviour, read Tom Bower's biography of Robert Maxwell, Mandarin, 1988). To me there is a high degree of inconsistency in all this. If you want to provide exceptionally fine customer service, I believe that it is critical that this is reflected in your own manners, in dealing with your customers in a polite and respectful way.

I am really dealing with nuances here, but they are important nuances. I know a lot of friendly people, but occasionally when they write to me their letters come across as cold and matter of fact. They have not seized the opportunity of injecting one scrap of warmth into the letter. So I begin to wonder, have I upset them? I haven't, of course, but even so I feel uneasy at the unfriendly tone.

That is the problem with discourtesy. People begin to feel devalued, as if they were not respected. A discourteous person seems to display an attitude that he or she is superior to the other person.

Discourtesy thus reveals something about a person. Sometimes it is no more than thoughtlessness – for example, inadvertently forgetting to say 'Please' or 'Thank you'. Other times it is a reflection of how you value other people, and how you value yourself.

There should be no differentials in the extension of courtesy. Whomever the person, whatever that person's station in life, their status, their origin, their qualifications – all should be extended the

---

COMMON COURTESIES

- If someone takes you out to lunch, always write and say thank you

- Always open the door for other people, no matter who they are

- Never break a promise, always do as you say you are going to do (say, when you promise to send some information, send it)

- Offer visitors refreshments in reception

- Always pour the tea for the other person first

- Don't use language that in any way could offend

- Allow other people to go first (say, in a queue)

- Allow people to complete what they're saying, don't interrupt

- Put yourself out for people (such as by showing them the way)

- Remember people's names and use them in conversation ('You remember, Margaret, when you were at ...' is better than 'You remember when we were at ...'

- Always reply to letters. It doesn't matter who the people are, if they take the trouble to write to you, always reply

- Don't send someone else to collect a visitor at reception, take the trouble to go and greet them yourself – and make them feel welcome

- Always return telephone calls

- Never be late for meetings

- Always show respect for the other person

- If something goes wrong, always apologize to the other person

- Never take anything for granted (say, always ask permission to use someone's time, or facilities, etc.)

---

same courtesy. It is just as important to be courteous to an unshaven, unemployed tramp as to a member of royalty. Personally I react a little to the complicated etiquette one has to perform when meeting royalty. Etiquette, after all, is no more than a formalization of courtesy. I am not against bowing and scraping *per se*, just as long as everyone bows and scrapes towards each other. Making that the preserve and privilege of royalty alienates me. But I digress.

Many senior executives, though, behave in a 'royalist' manner, expecting special courtesies that are not extended to more humble people like me. Why address the Chairman as 'Chairman' when everyone else is called by their first names? Often it comes down to simple courtesies like greeting people in the corridor or when passing reception first thing in the morning. Do you go out of the way to say 'Good morning' to the Managing Director and then neglect to do so to the security guards at the entrance? Don't they command respect, too? Aren't they people?

Some of us tend to pass each other by on the street and look the other way. We forget to acknowledge people. I have seen directors interrupt conversations to speak to senior people and completely ignore the front-line people the senior managers were talking to.

Bad manners and discourtesy are everywhere, but, as a boss, it won't do you any good if you behave in this way. You need to demonstrate your respect for people by extending them the everyday courtesies you were taught as a child but are in danger of neglecting now.

PRINCIPLE:
Respect and equal treatment for all.

PRACTICE:
Discipline yourself to extend courtesies to every-one and take a pride in this.

As soon as possible, seize the opportunity to feed back to your people how you see their efforts.

Double-check what people say to you by giving them a summary of what you think they said.

28

Use experts

Never do it yourself if an expert can do it better.

The days when an organization had on tap a reservoir of employees possessing every expertise imaginable are rapidly disappearing. Ideally, you would pick up the phone and find the company's expert on legal matters, or on personnel advice, or who could help you out on an IT problem, or could talk you through the latest financial forecast. Today, the likelihood is that these people will not be employees of your company but will instead sell you their services, and you will be able to select from an increasingly wide choice of expertise.

As financial constraints rain down on you, the luxury of having a pool of experts within your own area of responsibility will no longer be feasible. In future, expertise will have to be purchased in carefully measured timeslots.

One instinctive reaction to all this would be to attempt to do everything yourself – for example, your own PR, or your own graphic design, or your own accounts, and, thus, get everything on the cheap. This, though, would be an unwise move. Why waste your own time doing things the experts could do much better? A consultant who charges £2000 a day may *seem* expensive, but is, in fact, far cheaper than employing a specialist of lesser expertise for £40 000 per year who then creates work to fill the time and justify their own existence. You can stop using a consultant very quickly, if necessary, but it is much more difficult to stop using an expert who is permanently employed with you.

The key task is to identify the type of help you need to reach your goals and then, over a period of time, develop a network of experts who can provide that help. Selection will be the difficult part. Every expert you meet will make out that they have *the* approach that will solve your problem. When you dangle the prospect of an assignment in front of them, few are honest enough to admit that they cannot help.

Furthermore, as you get on to various firms' mailing lists, you will be inundated with letters from consultants and professionals prospecting for work. Invariably they will be accompanied by glossy brochures and leaflets. The temptation is to bin them right away. Don't! Spend a second or two studying each one. Occasionally one will catch your eye and you might want to pursue the enquiry a little

---

DON'Ts AND DOs – SOME EXPERT EXAMPLES

- *Don't* produce your own brochures and leaflets
- *Do* use expert copywriters and graphic designers
- *Don't* run your own training programmes
- *Do* use professional trainers
- *Don't* do your own advertising
- *Do* use professional advertising companies
- *Don't* do your own finances
- *Do* use a qualified accountant
- *Don't* conduct your own surveys
- *Do* use experienced survey firms
- *Don't* form your own opinion on matters of law
- *Do* consult a lawyer as early as possible
- *Don't* do your own secretarial work
- *Do* use a professional secretary
- *Don't* organize major conferences yourself
- *Do* use a conference organizer
- *Don't* facilitate your own awayday sessions
- *Do* use a first-class facilitator

---

further. As a matter of courtesy, always reply personally to people who take the trouble to write to you personally.

The best way to select experts is the tried and tested common-sense method of reputation and word of mouth. When you're running up against a certain type of problem, discuss it with as many people as you can. Ask them whether they know of anybody who could help. Then approach the suggested people for an exploratory chat.

Don't assume that you always have to go to external sources for your supply of expertise, though. It is worth developing the network within your own organization and even among your own people. By helping your people develop expertise in their own jobs, you develop the potential of making this expertise available to other sections, departments, and outside companies. To sustain the reputation of your section (or department) you do need to have a constant flow of experts in and out of it. This will prove highly motivating for your people as they will then be exposed to a wider range of situations in which they can develop their skills further.

PRINCIPLE:
You cannot do everything yourself.

You cannot be expert in most things.

PRACTICE:
Hunt out the experts who might be able to help you in the future and develop good relationships with them. Lend them your expertise when they need it. It will be reciprocated.

29

Eliminate favouritism

Favouritism divides! Be scrupulous about treating everyone equally.

Few of us admit to favouritism, but it is surreptitious. We send out signals all the time indicating those we favour and those we don't.

Life would be horrendously monotonous if we all liked the same type of person – we would all be seeking the same partner in marriage. So, the exciting reality is that we are all different and like different types of people. In a social environment this might be fine, but in the world of management it can be incredibly dangerous.

People react adversely to discrimination, and favouritism is a subtle form of discrimination. It is difficult to hide: most people have incredibly sensitive antennae and will quickly become aware when one person is 'in' with the boss while another is not. In fact, many bosses develop reputations for confiding in and seeking the advice of a series of people who can be 'in' one day and 'out' the next.

In trying to eliminate favouritism, any boss is presented with two opposing principles. The first is to be objective, fair, and not to discriminate between people. The second, opposing, principle is that a boss should be a human being and act accordingly. Most of us act in accordance with our likes and dislikes.

However, the two opposing principles can be reconciled by the simple expedient of concentrating on what you *like* about each person in the team – without exceeding the bounds of proper behaviour. Don't concentrate on what you *dislike* about a person. Try to discover the good points of people around you and use these as a basis for developing your relationship with them. Ensure you give each a fair share of your time and, similarly, by taking each

---

A TALE OF TWO MAFIAS

This is an extract from a conversation that took place during a workshop run by the author.

Participant 1

'The trouble with our senior management team is that it is not a team. There are two groups within it. The first is two or three men who go drinking with the boss at lunchtime. He likes his pint and so do these other three. They talk 'shop' at lunchtime and that's where all the important decisions seem to be made. The rest of us are left out of it. Most of the women on the team and one or two of the men don't like drinking at lunchtime. So we feel as if we are outsiders, we don't know what's going on, we don't seem to get involved in the important decisions.'

Participant 2

'We have the same type of situation at our office. Our boss is a heavy smoker, yet we work in a non-smoking building with dedicated smoking rooms. Our boss regularly goes to the smoking room at 10.45 a.m. for a fag. One or two of the others who also smoke go there with her and they chat away. We feel left out, too. Unless we're prepared to brave the fug in the smoking room we rarely get to see our boss, she never holds meetings for the rest of us, and she doesn't bother to let us know what's going on. It seems we have a smoking mafia here.'

---

equally into your confidence. Furthermore, ensure that any rewards (tangible or intangible, direct or indirect) are distributed with scrupulous fairness. Remember, too, that a small word of praise can be an effective reward.

In trying to eliminate favouritism you have to be extremely careful on the issue of sexual attractiveness. Some bosses will be drawn to the most sexually attractive people in their team, even going out of their way to recruit sexually attractive people. Other bosses overcompensate by *avoiding* sexually attractive people for fear that their motives will be misinterpreted when attempting everyday contact. It is an area fraught with difficulty and most bosses with any element of sexual drive will have to walk a tightrope when dealing with people they find attractive.

'IN' WITH THE BOSS

'I don't get on too well with my boss. I'm not sure why – we are just not comfortable in each other's presence. However, one of my colleagues seems to have a way with him, knows how to make him laugh. I don't. One day he came down to see my colleague, who was chatting to me at the time. He interrupted our conversation and raised some issue with her. Not once during the five minutes he was talking with her did he acknowledge my presence. He totally ignored me, didn't even say "Hello".'

'She is always in the boss' office with him. It must be hours every week. The rest of us never get a look in. I think he's got a soft spot for her. In my worst moments I just wonder if something else is going on.'

There is no easy answer to the process of eliminating favouritism except to continually challenge yourself on your own thoughts, your own motives, and your own behaviours to ensure that your own preferences for individuals do not show through at the expense of others around you.

PRINCIPLE:
Fairness, equality, and objectivity in the way you treat everyone around you.

PRACTICE:
Continually challenge yourself on your own behaviours with other people.

Always ask yourself the question 'Am I giving preference to anyone'? Unless you can openly justify a 'yes' answer to your people, the answer should always be 'no'.

30

Eyeball people on difficult issues

The measure of any manager lies in the eyes.

This morning I was in a meeting with a senior executive (let's call him Brian). A month ago, he had taken over responsibility for a major service operation in a large organization. His predecessor had failed to achieve some critical operational targets and had been transferred elsewhere to 'an important project'.

The discussion with Brian centred on the seven members of his management team, only one of whom he seemed to have confidence in. He confessed to having a particular problem with Marion, whom he saw as not committed and reacted negatively to his demands for information. Apparently she saw him as 'interfering' all the time. The situation was getting so desperate that he was thinking of transferring her out of the team. I questioned whether he had eyeballed her on her lack of commitment, on her attitudinal problems. 'I've told her many times what I require', he responded assertively. However, it was clear that he had not told her what he had told me, and that was his real feelings about her. He simply had not come clean with her about the way he really saw her.

Many managers are escapologists. They escape from facing up to difficult people and honestly expressing their views to them. They prefer to moan about them behind their backs, or send 'hints' in 'prickly' memos (the famous innuendo that the reader has to discover by reading between the lines).

Facing up to people and eyeballing them on perceived deficiencies is one of the most difficult tasks for any boss. The process can be

---

THE DAY I RAN DOWN MY BOSS

'Within a few weeks of joining the team, I attended my first team meeting. My boss raised a fairly important issue and asked for comments. I said nothing. He suggested an approach to dealing with the issue. Again I said nothing, although I felt his approach was wrong. There was mild dissent from other team members, but, even so, my boss pushed ahead with his approach and informed the team at the end of the meeting of his decision.

We broke for lunch and I went off to the canteen with my team-mates. As we queued up for our meals, I began running my boss down, telling my team-mates how stupid he was to push such an approach. I really rubbished him.

To my horror, I turned round to see my boss had arrived in the queue behind me. He had heard every word I said. I trembled, but said nothing. I collected my lunch and remained quiet while I ate it.

At 2.00 p.m. after returning from lunch, the phone rang in my office. It was my boss. He asked me to go and see him. "This is it", I thought, I'm going to be fired now.

My boss sat me down the other side of his desk and eyeballed me. "I heard every word you said at lunch," he told me, "now forget it!"

I started grovelling, making lame excuses. He stared at me, hammered the table and said "When I say forget it, I mean it!"

He was one of the best bosses I ever had. He taught me never to talk behind his back, to have the courage of facing up to him on any issue.'

---

exceptionally painful and most managers shy away from it, fearing an emotional reaction.

Inevitably, you cannot eyeball people on every little problem – indeed, a key attribute of any great boss is being tolerant of imperfections – but if these imperfections are of such a magnitude as to threaten your results, then you must do something about them. What you must do is eyeball the person concerned.

Amazingly, most people *want* to know where they stand with their boss. The worst bosses, I am told time and time again, are those who are not straight with their people, who say one thing one day and another the next.

The skill in eyeballing people is to examine your underlying motives in facing up to that person. Is it to make the person feel bad? Is it to punish the person?

The answer to all of these questions should be 'No'. If you have a problem with another person, your motive should always be to help that person overcome that problem. Eyeballing, therefore, is all about giving constructive feedback to someone to help them do their job more effectively.

Most people are unaware of the impact of their own attitudes and behaviours on others. Many are not even conscious of their own attitudes and how they show through. So, holding up a mirror to a person's face is one of the most important things you must do as a boss. We all need to look inside ourselves.

People will respect any boss who sits down with them for an eyeballing session to provide honest feedback.

PRINCIPLE:
Openness and honesty. Immediate action.

PRACTICE:
When you have a problem with a person, sit down with that person and inform that person of the problem, eyeball to eyeball.

31

Look the part (remain calm, don't panic)

What's on the surface is just as important as what's hidden below.

Here's a terrible dilemma: you want to be one of them, you can't be one of them. Just to develop understanding and cooperation, you need to get as close as possible, but you can't get too close.

Some radicals would do away with the boss completely and go for self-managing groups. But, even self-managing groups will find a leader, and that leader will set him or herself apart in some small way. Ideally, there is no need for authority, it should be shared about equally. In practice, though, the need will always be there.

You have to face up to the reality that you are the boss and as such you will be different to the rest. Your people will want to look up to you, to respect you, trust you, obtain your support. They will expect you to make tough decisions and confront issues.

Surprisingly, they will also expect you to behave like a boss, to look the part. It's not just a matter of dress but also a matter of how you go about things. Looking the part is about how you walk, how you talk, how you smile. It's about whose eye you catch and the tone of your voice. It's about how you react to a crisis – whether you remain calm or panic. It's about the state of your office – whether it's cluttered with paper or scrupulously clean and tidy. It's about attention to detail and whether you bother about dirty windows, filthy toilets, and overflowing waste-paper baskets. It's about appearance. Appearance influences. It has an impact on your credibility. It's what people (rightly or wrongly) judge you by.

You might have a brilliant brain, but express yourself in a gobbledegook manner, which alienates. You might be incredibly wise, but have offensive stains on your jacket. You might be the sincerest person imaginable, but be *so* full of smiles that people distrust you. You might walk so fast your people are scared to approach you or talk so slow people get bored waiting for the point. You might flap under pressure or lose your temper when tired. You might be so full of confidence that your people lose confidence in you because you never appear to listen and always think you're right.

Appearances can be deceptive. Don't aim to deceive. Ensure that the surface can be reconciled with what's below. To be the boss, you must *look* the part, because you *are* the part.

Take a look around you, at your own boss, at other bosses. What do you see? How do you judge them? Do they meet your expectations? Do they look the part? Your people will be answering these questions in relation to you.

It is critical that you take care with the way you present yourself. Always be conscious of how you dress and the impact it will have on other people. A loosened tie, unkempt hair, creased clothes, an ill-fitting jacket, a stained shirt or blouse, dirty shoes, bitten fingernails – all will tell people a lot. Don't think they won't notice, they will. As a boss, they will try to 'read' you carefully. They will read you through your appearance as well as your words and actions.

Actions are equally important. Your people will judge you by every little thing you do. Looking the part is all about whether you leave your office door open or not, about who gets the coffee, who goes first in the queue. It is about how you greet people as you walk through the open-plan area. It is about how you answer the telephone as well as the style of the letters you send.

Looking the part is about sending signals to other people about yourself. Too many bosses are totally unaware of the signals they send, the body language, the innuendoes, the hidden meanings.

Try to develop a total awareness of how you are and how people see you. Practise observing other people (in buses, trains, shops, restaurants, crowds) when they are not aware you are watching. You will see things about people they never see themselves. Most people get totally immersed in themselves, channelling all their thoughts and energies into narrow directions, totally unaware of the broader impact of their behaviour. In other words, people are always giving away tell-tale signs about themselves, often signs they want to hide, signs that have a negative impact on others.

This is not an argument for total control (people who are too controlled often alienate). But it is an argument for increased awareness of yourself as a person, and that means awareness of how you look, how you behave and the impact you have on others. Always feel free to express yourself as a human being – this is not irreconcilable with expressing yourself as a boss.

In looking the part, avoid being false by acting out a role that is not you. When you look the part, it has to be you, you have to mean it, not pretend.

PRINCIPLE:
Ensuring consistency between you, as a real person, and how you appear as a boss.

PRACTICE:
Maintain a high standard of dress and personal appearance as a reflection of your own high standards of work (even if the required dress is casual).

Avoid behaviour that lowers people's confidence in you (don't demean yourself).

Be conscious of how you behave and the impact your behaviour has on others.
Be natural, not artificial.

32

Be on the ball (know what's important, not what's unimportant)

Only those on the ball can score goals.

Too many managers become immersed in the unimportant, devoting unnecessary energy and time to issues that could be handled more effectively by their people.

There are others who never seem to know what's going on, who don't seem to be in touch with reality, who are forever caught unawares, who plead ignorance or express surprise when confronted with something they should know about.

Every organization buzzes with 'live' issues, things going on now, happenings and events. Some are trivial, some are of major importance. Great bosses have incredibly sensitive antennae and are always aware of what's happening. That doesn't mean to say they are involved with everything, but they will know what's going on and what's important. They will know that Jenny has just gone into labour, that Ravinda's father is in hospital, that Luke is going for his finals next week. They will know that the line stopped last night and three hour's production was lost. They will know that the company's bid for the Harvey contract will be decided next week, that the company is thinking of upgrading the computer system, that there is to be a major initiative on improving quality.

Great bosses know what their people need to know and make sure they are the first to get the necessary information. Great bosses know what genuinely interests their people and go out of their way to sustain that interest.

To be on the ball requires five simple management skills, these are shown in the box below.

KEY BALL SKILLS

1 The ability to prioritize certain types of information
2 The ability to go out and about and seek that priority information (it never comes on a plate – despite most organizations' elaborate attempts to systematize this process of communication)
3 Relationships skills (the ability to get people to give you priority information before you ask for it)
4 The ability to sense what information your people and your own boss need as well as what interests them
5 The ability to quickly and effectively communicate that information

---

From time to time, however, you will find that, no matter how hard you tried, you will be caught out – you will not have the answer, you will not be in the know. For example, you might be in an important meeting with the Chief Executive and she levels at you a curler of a question about why you are overspent on the travel budget. It just so happens that you have been away on a trip for the last five days, were late in this morning because your wife was ill, and you had to take the kids to school. Therefore, you haven't had an opportunity to look at the weekly financial statements. Don't worry, be honest. Tell the Chief Executive you don't know, but will find out very quickly.

Too many managers *pretend* to be on the ball. They cover up by bluffing their responses to difficult questions. Eventually they get caught out.

Being on the ball means that information is communicated through the proper channels, so you don't find out from a *customer* that the delivery has been delayed but from your own despatch department, you don't find out from your *own people* that your boss is leaving. Conversely, it means giving your own boss and your own people important information before they find out from other sources.

Being on the ball means being alert to everyone's needs, being alert to what's happening in the organization. It also means focusing clearly on the direction in which you want to go and ensuring you have adequate information to help you get there.

Being on the ball also means being up to date with the latest technology, the latest developments. It means avidly reading the latest reports, professional and technical journals as well as talking with the experts. It means visiting exhibitions and attending seminars.

People like to have a boss who is 'in the know', who has an excellent feel for what's going on in the organization and beyond.

The converse of being on the ball is being ignorant.

PRINCIPLE:
Progress is dependent on the possession of specified priority information.

PRACTICE:
Practise the five key skills for being on the ball.

33

Show your customers around

*It is not just a question of what you make,
but what you are made of.*

Never hide anything from your customers. The more you hide, the more suspicious they will become, and the greater will be the risk of losing business through an erosion of trust.

There is a myth that doing business is an adversarial contest between customer and supplier, that it's about wheeling and dealing to extract the best price at the expense of others. Negotiating prowess becomes the order of the day in a macho world where lines are spun and big fish are hooked.

In reality, business is about people, and when dealing with people you have two choices. You either work on a basis of trust or on one of distrust. You either assume your customers are with you or on the other side of the line. It is 'all of us together' versus 'us and them'.

My preference is clear. I believe in partnerships. I believe in working on a basis of trust. That means being totally open and honest with your customers. It means 'open book' accounting (showing your customers around your accounts). It means having nothing to hide (showing your customers around your location). It means communicating the truth and nothing but the truth. Such freedom of expression means introducing customers to your people and encouraging your people to say whatever they like. No constraints. No censorship. No off-limit topics.

Those who fear the truth will never show their customers around.

They will be frightened of what their customers might find, the games that are being played, the short-cuts, the massaged figures, the outspoken dissidents, the dirty linen.

You cannot create credibility from surface reflection. What's under the surface is of fundamental importance in achieving a high reputation in the eyes of your customers. You must lift off the gloss of your sales promotions and fine brochures to reveal the real thing. You must show your customers around so that they can experience it direct.

It's all too easy to say that the product should speak for itself. Business is more than selling a product whose intrinsic qualities explicitly meet customer requirements. It's about a total experience. It's about relationships in the purchase and supply of that product. It's about confidence and trust. Customers need to have trust that if things go wrong there will be people around to ensure effective reparation. They need to trust that the people who put it together can be relied on to give their best.

Then there is the question of motivation. People who make the product or deliver the service like to meet the people who receive and use it. Pride is a powerful motivator and can be readily generated when customers are shown around. Standards are raised, improvements made when you know the people (customers) whose decisions determine your future. Floors are swept, reception areas are refurbished, and even factories modernized when the all-important customers make their tours.

Showing customers around protects against narrow-mindedness and complacency. You come to find out what they think, what it really means to use your products – and they find out what it's really like to produce them. This mutual understanding is invaluable in securing commitment. The relationships that are struck up provide a powerful force in driving the business forward. The customers will know better who to turn to when there's a problem, they will be able to put a face to a name. And with face and name in mind, your people will give ten times more attention to your customers than if they were just numbers on a computer printout. It's the human element of business. It's the most compelling argument for operating on the basis of trust, and so obvious, too!

Inevitably there is a note of caution. You can become a victim of your own success, spending all your time showing customers around. You then risk neglecting the operation that produces the excellent products they demand. A balanced and controlled approach must be the answer. Encourage your customers to come to visit you and your people to meet them, but do it in a way that fits in with your operation requirements. Have guided tours if there is a high demand. Share the responsibility for hosting customers around equally among your people. Choose between a formal and informal approach, depending on the type of business you are in.

In summary, you need to maximize the opportunities for your customers to visit you where you work, to show them around, to see how you go about things, and also to meet people.

If you have neglected to do so recently, get on the phone now and fix some dates for a number of your customers to come to see your operation. You can entice them with a nice lunch, but the real draw will be for them to meet your people and to get to know them.

This need applies even if you only have internal customers. If you run the personnel department, have your line management customers come around. If you run the post room, encourage the people who use your services to take an interest in how you operate by showing them the system.

Get your customers involved – it pays dividends.

PRINCIPLE:
Openness and honesty.

Taking an interest in your customers.

Working together with customers.

Motivation through pride.

PRACTICE:
Issue invites today for some of your customers to come to have a look around and meet your people.

34

Read books and go on seminars

To be successful we need to be stimulated, frequently.

It is all too easy to close in on ourselves and allow our view of the world to become narrower and narrower. We tend to see the world through company glasses. We begin to believe that *our* way is the *only* way, that it is *the* right way. The risk is that we delude ourselves that we know everything, that we know best, that there is no better way. We develop an inclination to reject other ways as inferior, as ignorant.

As we become immersed in our daily routines, we lose perspective, our sense of what is proper becomes distorted. We cease to question and challenge what is going on, accepting ineffective ways because that has always been the way. We get to the stage where we have no idea that other people can do things differently and probably more effectively.

It is essential, therefore, that any boss gets exposure to what other organizations and other people are doing. It's a matter of keeping up to date with competitive practice, of finding out what's happening in America and elsewhere.

Organizations frequently suffer major learning disabilities, does yours? Or more pertinently have you read Peter Senge's excellent book *The Fifth Discipline* (Doubleday, 1990), about the art and practice of the learning organization? To quote from the book: 'In most companies that fail, there is abundant evidence in advance that the firm is in trouble. This evidence goes unheeded, however, even when individual managers are aware of it. The organization as a whole cannot recognize impending threats, understand the implications of those threats, or come up with alternatives'.

Over the last three decades, there have been consistent predictions about the breakup of large bureaucratic organizations. In 1973, E. F. Schumacher wrote that 'people can be themselves only in small, comprehensible groups' in his influential work *Small is Beautiful* (Blond & Briggs, 1973). Nine years later, John Naisbitt indicated in *Megatrends* (Warner Books, 1982) that one of the key trends for the future was the decentralization of large organizations. In the 1990s, Tom Peters in *Liberation Management* (Macmillan, 1992) says a similar thing: 'The massive, vertically integrated enterprise ... is dead'.

You don't even have to read management books to discover this message. If you want evidence of the destructive power of huge bureaucracies where people are told what to think, how to behave, then read Jung Chang's excellent book *Wild Swans* (HarperCollins, 1991).

The main point is simple, and, again, it is common sense. To make progress as a boss, you must seek and read books that stimulate your thinking, spark new ideas, enable you to reflect on your own situation, and, overall, help you learn about what is going on elsewhere. Having said that, there are thousands of books being published each year. To select the most stimulating ones, you need to exchange views with your colleagues, to study the reviews in the papers, to get up to date through professional journals. What's more, you need to attend external seminars at least twice a year. While your initial inclination might be to bin the mass of mailshots entering your in-tray, try to sift through them and select those that excite your interest, that are going to give you a fresh perspective. It is worth investing a few hundred pounds in going to hear the top speakers. Not only will you benefit from what they have to say, but you will also meet other delegates with whom you can share experiences.

Reading books and attending seminars is all about keeping an open mind, being prepared to accept new ideas. The people who make progress in life are those who have a thirst for learning and are able to relate that learning to their own workplace. Furthermore, the process of reading, learning, and stimulation will result in you sustaining positive, enthusiastic attitudes about the future. People who close their minds tend to become cynical and defeatist.

It's a discipline. Try to have one business-related book 'on the go' at any one time. Take notes as you read (and also when you attend seminars). Develop an avid interest in what other people are reading. Discuss books, with colleagues, with your people, with your boss. Use extracts from books, or notes from seminars you've attended as a basis for discussion with the people you work with. Try always to relate what you learn to developing your own approach at work.

PRINCIPLE:
Keeping an open mind.
The need for continual learning.
The need for stimulus.

PRACTICE:
Try to read one stimulating book (related directly or indirectly to management) every month.

Attend at least two external seminars every year.

Listen to others, and seek out their recommendations on books to read and seminars to attend.

35

Think bottom line

The harsh and inescapable reality of business life is that without a positive bottom line you wouldn't have a job.

The larger the organization, the greater the tendency for managers and their people to forget that there is an ultimate goal. Survival and growth can only be achieved through a sound bottom line on the financial statement.

Too many managers see their organizations as an inexhaustible reservoir of resources. In pursuit of their dreams for their own departments, they wage constant battle with the centre to spend more on staff, training, equipment, marketing, and so on.

THE BOTTOM LINE

Every boss should see his or her area of responsibility as a 'business unit' in which the value of outputs exceeds the value of inputs (where inputs include overheads and central charges).

The difference is added value.

ADDED VALUE = VALUE OF OUTPUTS – VALUE OF INPUTS

No boss can be divorced from the reality that every pound of expenditure must, ultimately, generate more than one pound of revenue. Requests to have an additional administrator costing £15 000 per year can only be justified if it can be shown that more than £15 000 of revenue will be generated as a result.

The same principle applies to every item of expenditure. A business trip costing £500 is only of value if there is a probability that it will result in additional revenue for the organization.

Inevitably, in deciding on expenditure the wise boss will take a view on the long-term benefits as well as the short-term ones. Indirect benefits also have to be gauged. For example, it can be demonstrated (see the report in *Fortune*, 22 March 1993, or the article by Michael Porter, *Director*, April 1990) that organizations that invest in training on an ongoing basis tend to be more successful in the long term than those who don't.

To enable managers to think about the bottom line, more and more organizations are now decentralizing into business units, where each manager has real accountability for producing a set of outputs (measured financially) with a given set of inputs.

It is a cliché to say that you should treat company money as if it were your own. However, really successful bosses encourage their people to think this way. They encourage their people to assess their own success against the unit's bottom line.

Ultimately, everyone's activities at work should be geared towards enhancing that bottom line. The best bosses, therefore, ensure that all their people understand how their contribution affects it.

It does mean that every individual has to be clearly informed about the current situation regarding outputs and inputs, and the impact of their efforts on the organization's financial results.

BOTTOM LINE IMPACT	
	Impact
Putting yourself out for potential customers	**Orders gained**
Quick follow-up to enquiry	**Orders gained**
Offering that little extra at no extra cost	**Orders gained**
Keeping customers informed	**Orders retained**
Extending a warm welcome at reception	**Orders retained**
Keeping the premises clean	**Orders retained**
Appearing indifferent to customers' needs	**Lost orders**
Failure to answer telephone calls	**Lost orders**
Failure to reply to letters	**Lost orders**

The bottom line provides a clear focus for measuring real progress. If you lose sight of it, the risk is that things will get out of control, expenditure soars, and profit margins decline. Great bosses, therefore, relate everything they do to the bottom line, and so do their people.

PRINCIPLE:
A healthy financial bottom line is essential for an organization's long-term existence.

PRACTICE:
Think bottom line all the time.

Always examine the impact of your decisions on the bottom line.

Encourage your people to think the same way.

36

Manage in ignorance

Ignorance can be a virtue, not a sin.

Insecurity is all too pervasive in many managers. They like to know everything going on, and waste a lot of time trying to find out. They get totally immersed in detail. The saying goes 'they can't see the wood for the trees'.

It's a deep-rooted vulnerability suffered by many. They don't want to be caught out. They want to be the first to know – that way they can be the first to tell. So, they demand long-winded reports, masses of data, and analyses. They are on the phone getting up to date every five minutes. As they delve for more and more useless information, they create an aura of being incredibly busy and, of course, incredibly important.

The saying goes 'information is power'. Insecure managers delude themselves into thinking that by acquiring more information they will become more powerful. Back to the bad old word of 'empowerment' (despite my aversion to jargon and buzz-words, the term 'empowerment' is useful at times!). If you really believe in empowering your people, then you have to believe that they are going to have all the useful information to enable them to do their jobs effectively. As soon as you demand this information for yourself, presumably to enable you to make decisions, you effectively 'disempower' your people.

You should have the information that enables you to make decisions, which enables you to monitor what is going on, which is required by your own bosses. As you push decision making down the hierarchy, the emphasis will be more on having regular monitoring information. It is natural to take an interest in what your people are doing and not unreasonable to receive a regular report from them on their progress. That report can be daily, weekly, or monthly, depending on the nature of your business. It should be stressed that the information provided in the regular report should be geared specifically to the achievement of your unit's overall goals. All other information is irrelevant.

To be honest, do you really need to see the holiday schedules, the absentee statistics, detailed analyses of individual machine performance? Do you really need to know who has been attending which meetings and what was discussed? Do you really need to know what the Managing Director said to Jack when he did his weekly walk around? Do you really need to know where Zoë is at this very moment or what Fred is doing about the typing problem?

Take an interest in what's going on, provide support when necessary, but don't let yourself become immersed in masses of information. Manage in ignorance!

All this does require a high degree of trust, of course. You will have to trust your people to keep you informed on vital matters. They will need to understand that if there is a serious threat to fulfilling an important customer's order due to a plant breakdown that you need to learn from them rather than from the Managing Director who has just had the irate customer on the line.

Managing this kind of ignorance really is bliss. It does allow you to go and do very important things – like meeting customers, like discussing last night's television with your people, like thinking through the long-term direction the unit should take, like liaising with your colleagues in other departments, like undertaking some training – or even giving some.

In essence, managing in ignorance is letting your people get on and do their jobs without too much interference, trusting that they are going to contact you if something goes wrong, or if they need your help, or if they want to discuss the possibility of making some improvements.

A further advantage of managing in ignorance is that you get home earlier, see more of your family, and have more time to exercise and keep fit.

It is worth trying, so start tomorrow! You will find that even if you *don't* know what's going on, the unit will not collapse under the weight of your ignorance. In fact, it will probably run more effectively as you won't be distracting people with your silly demands for useless information. You'll find it an interesting if not exhilarating experience. So will your people.

Don't worry if your own boss catches you out with a question of detail. Bosses tend to be more reasonable these days and most are prepared to wait five minutes while you go and retrieve the answers to their questions. It might be helpful if you explain why you are so ignorant. They might learn from it and you can both benefit accordingly.

As a boss, keep in touch with the important things at work, but, as for the detail, ignore it.

PRINCIPLE:
To be effective, the information you require should be prioritized.

PRACTICE:
Resist the temptation of finding out about every-thing that's going on.

Concentrate on the priorities.

37

Make it happen

The ability to turn difficult problems into easy solutions.

One of the afflictions of modern-day management is talk. There is too much consultation, too many meetings, too many steering groups and working parties. It seems that everyone has to be involved with everything. The end result is obvious. Nothing happens! It is impossible sometimes to get two people to agree, let alone 10 or 20. Trying to elicit a decision from 20 people is hugely more difficult than trying to elicit a decision from two. And trying to obtain a decision from two people is vastly more difficult than obtaining it from one.

The great bosses cut through all the claptrap. They crack problems others thought insurmountable. They make decisions on those cloudy issues where the mist of dissent swirls around and where the occasional shaft of light is met with suspicion.

Making it happen is all about throwing logic, analysis, and argument out of the window. It is all about taking a risk and following your gut instinct. Sometimes a cursory study of a problem people have agonized over for months will yield an obvious solution. Many people won't agree with that solution and that's why no decision has been made. The great bosses make the decision, give their reasons, and proceed. They take risks, knowing that they cannot please everyone all the time. They even risk being wrong. However, indecision about a festering problem is a greater sin than attempting to solve it and failing.

As a boss, you must develop the art of fixing problems, of making things happen. Look around at the people in your organization. You

---

BUILDING SENSE

'For five years our design engineers had been housed in temporary Terrapin buildings which they had been promised they would be out of in six months.

But the business had grown and the permanent buildings seemed to be full of people reluctant to release space to the design engineers. For five years the then Building Services Manager, who was responsible for accommodation, had been subjected to a barrage of complaints from the engineers. He always had one excuse or another for his inaction – the final one being that the decision was up with the Managing Director. As the Managing Director didn't want to get involved in detailed decisions about floor layouts and allocations of space, he put the papers into his pending tray and forgot about them.

The Building Services Manager retired and a new, young guy was recruited to take over from him. He listened carefully to the design engineers and then quickly studied the various options that had laid dormant for years. He made his decision and the engineers were out of the Terrapin within three months of him joining. There were some murmurs of dissent from the people who had to give up space, but, in the end, everything settled down well'.

---

will know at least one person who can be relied on to get something done, who never complains, no matter how difficult the task. You know who I am talking about! As a boss you need to be all of that person and more.

'Leave it to me, I'll see to it' should be your motto. Nothing should be too much trouble for you. Unless you are trying for the moon, most problems that come your way should be solvable. Consult, yes, but not for too long – you'll never get everyone to agree – then, make a decision and implement it. The solution will normally be obvious, but not if you try to please everyone.

BLOW SENSE

'During winters, the warehousemen had to work in freezing temperatures, stacking pallets and loading them on to trucks. For two years they complained to their Manager about a lack of heating. They were always fobbed off with answers like "We're looking into it".

One day last winter, at 2.00 a.m. in the morning, the temperature dropped to $-10°C$. With their hands and cheeks frozen, the warehousemen decided they had had enough. They went on strike, huddling in their rest room (the only room with a radiator).

Within one hour, the Duty Manager somehow managed to conjure up from nowhere a number of powerful blow-heaters. The warehousemen went back to work. If the strike had continued, the penalties to the company for non-delivery would have been exceptionally high.

"Why", asked one of them, "does it take a strike to get something done round here?" '

PRINCIPLE:
Bosses have to risk making difficult decisions to make things happen.

PRACTICE:
When you are unsure what to do and there are many conflicting arguments, follow your gut instinct and make a decision based on that.

38

Celebrate achievement

It's so much better to share in success than keep it to oneself.

The time you spend at work should be enjoyable, if not fun. It should even provide the occasional thrill when something outstanding has been achieved, whether it be on the home front or at work. Most people enjoy a sense of achievement from time to time. You see this most vividly in children who have just ridden a bicycle for the first time, or have just learned to swim. Why not reinforce the experience of success at work?

No organization can afford to stand still these days – progress has to be made on many fronts, in the face of fierce competition. So, there are ample opportunities to celebrate achievement. Go seek them out. Don't be embarrassed at the prospect of calling your people together and presenting an award to someone who's really made an outstanding contribution, or taking your team out for a Chinese meal when they've really worked hard and been successful in accomplishing a difficult task.

The opportunities for celebrating achievements are endless, and you shouldn't confine the celebrations to events that take place at work. It is also worth celebrating things that happen at home, for example births, engagements, and marriages.

The actual method of celebration is less important than the actual act of doing so. There is no need to spend a lot of money either. What your people will welcome is the fact that you have recognized their achievement, valued it, and done something about it. Your efforts will be highly motivational and spur your people on to even greater achievement.

CELEBRATIONS

(Mix and match from the two columns below)

- Passing professional exams   Speech by boss
- Winning a contract   Night out
- Having a baby   Champagne after work
- Meeting productivity targets   Boss buys lunch
- Birthdays and anniversaries   Cards and cakes
- End of an excellent year   Dinner with spouses
- Promotion   Presentation of award
- Written compliment from customer   Display letter on noticeboard
- First-class results at training course   Certificate on wall
- End of a difficult project   River trip
- Section wins company award   Bonus for all
- Positive publicity   Exhibition of press-cuttings in reception
- Achieving 125 per cent of quota   Trip to Paris
- Winning at sport   Section presents trophy
- Getting a book published/article in a journal   Presentation of leather-bound edition

---

Again, when it comes to celebration, common sense should apply. Celebrate too often and the process will become devalued, will be seen as a routine. People will expect it, and this is dangerous. Celebration should never become routine. It should be spontaneous with minimal planning.

Don't just rely on your ideas to celebrate achievement. If someone has done something great, then involve their colleagues in producing at least one exciting idea to highlight and recognize the success.

Formal award schemes tend to suffer from the disadvantage that the panel will feel obliged to make a monthly or quarterly award for the sake of it, irrespective of whether anything worth while has been achieved or not. This risk is that they drag up some poor, undeserving person who has escaped an award over the last five years.

The keys are spontaneity and ensuring that the celebration is for genuine achievement.

So, seek out achievement. Just go and find it, then invent some unusual way of celebrating it. The more you celebrate, the more you will achieve.

PRINCIPLE:
Genuine recognition of success.

PRACTICE:
Make sure you know when your people are successful and make sure you find some appropriate way to celebrate that success.

39

Praise and encourage

The finest motivator is genuine praise while encouragement is the finest source of improvement.

Saying 'Thank you' is vitally important, but not enough. Praise has to be added.

You tend to say 'Thank you' for what people give, for the tasks they do, for the results they achieve. Praise is all about recognizing the valuable characteristics that enable people to deliver what's required and even more. You praise people's skills and then thank them for what they achieve with these skills.

It is easy to put people down, to criticize them for the way they go about things. Too many bosses find fault, drawing attention to minor mistakes and deficiencies in approach. As a result, people are led to believe, wrongly, that they are not good at this or weak in that. Traditional performance appraisal exacerbates the problem in that managers try hard to find defects (or even concoct them) in order to provide a balanced view of the individual. After all, no one can be perfect.

In reality, you cannot force criticism on to people. They will become defensive, will build up a shell at the surface that deflects any hints of shortcomings.

The way to seek improvement is to identify and value the good things people are doing and clearly demonstrate that you recognize these. It must be genuine recognition and cannot be too frequent.

Praise goes hand in hand with encouragement. Through genuine praise people feel valued and will, therefore, be encouraged to seek improvement to further enhance that value.

The starting point is to identify and praise people's good points. You should then go on to encourage them to add to these good points by making improvements. By being encouraged to take on bigger challenges, to develop their skills, to acquire new knowledge, to risk new experiences people add value to what they are. They grow in their own eyes as well as yours.

Encouragement is also to do with belief. Too often people lose belief in themselves. They are ground down by hostile organizations and unappreciative bosses who lead them to believe that they are worth relatively little and incapable of doing any more than what they're doing now. Our total culture, our corporate policies, and our own personal attitudes can generate an ethos that devalues the very people on whom we depend.

The great bosses genuinely value their people and demonstrate it with praise and encouragement. They have an intrinsic faith in the capability of their people to deliver. That faith extends to a belief in both groups of people as well as individuals. Often the belief a boss has in a person is greater than that a person has in himself (or herself).

Encouragement is all about developing an individual's personal self-belief. A belief that so and so *can* rise to the occasion or climb the highest mountain.

Without challenge, without encouragement, people invariably revert to the comfort and security of the mediocre present. It's the devil they know. It's their own self-imposed limitations to protect the all-embracing, but potentially suffocating, comfort and security. Too often we hear 'I could never do that' or 'It's impossible for me'. People find reasons for not venturing out, for not extending themselves. In doing this they limit themselves. A great boss helps remove the psychological limits people place on themselves. By the shrewd use of genuine praise and encouragement, these bosses reveal to people their inherent potential and the way it can be exploited.

The most potent phrase of encouragement and praise is 'You can do it, you've got what it takes!' It is a form of emotional support that is vital when anyone is facing a major test, whether it be an interview, an attempt to win an important contract, giving a keynote speech, confronting a hostile and abusive person, or whatever.

It is all too easy to lose sight of our own capabilities and potential. We need others around to help us recognize us for what we are. The great boss plays a crucial role in this. His (or her) job is to hold up a mirror to a person's face to reflect all the good points and to give confidence that with such attributes even greater things can be achieved.

It is worth studying the success of sports stars and how they benefit from excellent coaching and management. Invariably the coach or team captain has a critical role in providing a psychological support at crucial moments. The bad coach will say, 'Remember, don't drop the ball and remember not to lose your temper'. Such advice is negative and plays on deficiencies. The excellent coach will say, 'Remember, you can do it. You've done it before!' The encouragement plays on the positive beliefs players will have about themselves.

Praise and encouragement is about seeking out and accentuating the positive. It simultaneously reduces the fear of the negative.

PRINCIPLE:
Building on a person's good points.

PRACTICE:
Carefully consider the strengths of every single person for whom you are the boss and create an opportunity to praise that person's strengths.

When your people have to face up to major tests, provide positive emotional support. Demonstrate, through encouragement, your belief in their capability of meeting the test.

40

Create new things

Management is an art form. Art is all about creativity.

Managers would not be required if opportunities never arose, direction never required, problems never happened and failure never occurred.

Management is not about following procedures, maintaining systems (bureaucratic or technical) or adhering to rule books.

Nor is management a rational process in which a formula for success is identified and then followed. Nor is it a process in which a blatantly obvious set of logics is applied to organization and individual behaviour.

The worst managers are those who slavishly follow procedure, who defer consistently to organization dictat, who wait for orders and only respond to command.

The key attribute for great bosses is the ability to think for themselves, irrespective of propaganda emanating from above. Such thinking must be a process of creativity as opposed to thinking along predetermined lines established by a rational analysis of experience.

If there was a policy, procedure, system, or dictat for how to handle every conceivable problem that arose at work, life would be easy and we would all be amazingly successful. There can never be a prescription on how to seize an opportunity, or define direction, or avoid failure.

It's been said before, but the only certain thing about work is uncertainty. The uncertainty of the outside market, of economics, of politics. And uncertainty regarding the people within an organization, few of whom are that predictable that we know in advance how they are going to think and behave. Tom Peters asserts that we live in a crazy world, and that requires crazy people. He is probably right, although the word crazy is a little exaggerated.

Gone are the days of security and comfort in employment. Business is all about survival and success. There can never be any security or comfort about that.

It is increasingly difficult to bring a sense of order to this uncertain, if not crazy, world. However this is not a defeatist message. In fact the most exciting thing about the world we live in is that it requires an exceptional amount of creativity to survive and be successful. And that's positive creativity (negative creativity is a crime). Without continual creativity at work we become mediocre and risk failure as the competition creates ways of beating us at our own game.

For example, there might be a thousand textbooks on how to motivate people at work (this is one!), but not one of them can tell you *precisely* how to do it. At best, textbooks present examples and analysis of how others motivate (and are motivated) and lessons to be drawn from this. Such material can be of value in stimulating you to develop your own approach. Ultimately, however, the way you motivate must be your own creation, a product of your own learning and experience; it cannot be a simulation of another person's approach – far better to be original than to copy.

Another example relates to customer service. There might be a thousand textbooks on how to please your customers, how to provide exceptional customer service (I have written one!), but not one of them can tell you *precisely* how to do it. If they could, it would be easy and customer service would be exceptional everywhere. It isn't. Once again you must learn the lessons from the books, from others, and then create your own unique way of pleasing your customers.

The problems that come your way day by day will either be routine or exceptional. The routine problems are normally easy to solve. The real challenge for a great boss is to create solutions to the exceptional problems.

It is also to create opportunities – opportunities to survive and grow, beat the competition, sustain motivation, develop people, introduce new services and products, win new customers and retain old ones. Creativity at work is about continuous improvement, continuous change.

The reality is that there are fewer problems in life than opportunities. The biggest problem is that people don't see this. As we become obsessed with problems, opportunities pass us by, undetected.

As a boss you have an opportunity to be creative as soon as you walk through the door first thing in the morning. Repetition breeds complacency. So, create a new way of greeting your people, of involving them in what's going on. Solicit new ideas and pursue them. Find new ways of implementing ideas. Find new ways of selling your services, of expanding your business.

Creativity is not just about the big idea (the Apple Mac, Post-it notes, etc.) but also about the little things of everyday life (a new way of saying 'Thank you', a fresh approach to running meetings).

Bosses who are creative and innovative and encourage the same within their people will generate exceptional levels of performance from them. Creativity at work leads to excitement, interest, personal satisfaction, and reward.

Inevitably, and this is common sense, creativity has to be balanced with a degree of discipline – for example, in how money is spent, machinery is used, how people behave towards each other. But that should be obvious. The exercising of essential discipline is no excuse for not being creative.

PRINCIPLE:
Progress depends on creativity.

PRACTICE:
Avoid repetition and routine.

Try to do something different every day.

Encourage your people to be creative – and help them pursue their ideas.

Be conscious of the need to be creative and focus your energies on creating new things for the benefit of the business.

41

Keep your people up to date

To motivate people, you must keep alive their interest in the job and what goes on around them.

As a boss, you must always presume that your people are interested in what's going on and that they want to relate what they do to the overall success of the organization. One of your key tasks is to generate that interest, to prevent people from having such a narrow perspective that their only interest is in what happens after they finish work at 5.30 p.m.

Many jobs are of such a routine and repetitive nature that we struggle to imagine that there is any intrinsic interest in them. Yet interest *can* be generated, by connecting the routine to the non-routine, to the results of the company, to changes going on all around. It might be the achievement of weekly targets, or major new contracts won. It might be that Elizabeth has decided to retire next June, or that Harry is to be given a secondment to Personnel. It might be that the company is to install a new computer system to eliminate the drudgery of some of the clerical work currently undertaken.

We all depend on stimuli to keep us alive. There is much research evidence to suggest that stimuli deprivation retards the development of children. As adults we seek stimuli all the time. We go to the cinema, we try out new restaurants, we visit different places for holidays, we watch the news on television, we like to meet new people. We participate in sport and watch it because it gives us a buzz, it can be stimulating. In other words we love to get the adrenalin flowing from time to time, otherwise we retreat in a shell of introspection and mind-numbing boredom.

UPDATES

- **People changing jobs**
- **New products coming on stream**
- **Bids for new work**
- **Imminent publicity about the organization**
- **Planned training activities**
- **New investment in the company**
- **The purchasing of new equipment**
- **Success and failures (section, department, company)**
- **Planned changes to accommodation**
- **Improvements (all types)**
- **Latest initiatives**
- **Visitors to the section (or plant or office)**
- **Latest output figures (of section, department, company)**
- **Company results (weekly, monthly, quarterly, annually – sales volumes, profits, etc.)**

Work is no different. To sustain motivation, people need stimuli. Some of it can be self-generated, but a boss also has a vital role in the provision of such stimuli. Much of it comes from 'hot news', of getting to your people first with really interesting information. Failure to do so will result in gossip, rumour-mongering and speculation as people generate their own stimuli to alleviate the boredom of the routine.

As a boss, therefore, you need to ensure that you are completely au fait with what's going on. Furthermore, you need to develop incredibly sensitive antennae to the types of news that will really interest your people and discipline yourself to make sure you are the first to give it to them. By giving high priority to updating your

---

THE DAILY OPEN HOUSE

'I had a boss once who regularly had a 15-minute open house at 8.45 a.m. every morning. Coffee was served and anyone from the department could attend, irrespective of status. Nobody sat down. The purpose was to just go round the room and get an informal update on what had been going on over recent days. So, for example, if my boss had just returned from a trip, he would spend five minutes giving a summary on what had happened. If another person had been working on a problem, he or she would update the group on progress. If major changes were about to take place in the company, then our boss would alert us to them.

It was all very informal. No agenda, no minutes. All items were raised on an impromptu basis. Nobody was excluded from the meeting. It was a golden opportunity to have front-line people, such as the clerical staff and the telephonists, mix with the senior managers and the director. It worked well.'

---

people about what's going on, you demonstrate that you really value them, that you are really prepared to put yourself out to keep them informed.

The corollary to this is also true. If you make strenuous efforts to update your people, they will reciprocate. They won't attempt to pull the wool over your eyes or be economical with the truth. The process of updating is a two-way one. The more you do for your people to keep them informed, the more they will do for you. That's how motivation works.

To keep your people up to date, do not just rely on regular weekly or monthly briefing sessions – invariably these will come at the wrong time and not coincide with the release of important information. Place greater reliance on informal updates and impromptu meetings. Don't hesitate to pull your people together at short notice for a two-minute briefing on some news that has just broken.

PRINCIPLE:
Giving high priority to relevant information.

PRACTICE:
Get to know what really interests your people.

Put yourself out to make sure you keep your people up to date.

Try briefing your people on a daily basis.

Always make sure that you tell them first (rather than them finding out through the back door).

42

Listen to pop music, follow football, go to the cinema, and eat locally (acquire the tastes of your people)

Developing relationships with people at work is all about taking an interest in what interests them.

Contact between people is best established through identifying and pursuing areas of mutual interest. Your people will dismiss you as a narrow-minded bore if all you ever talk about is work. They won't be interested!

Strangely enough, if you want to talk about work, the most effective way is to start talking about things *other* than work, things that really interest your people. By homing in on innocuous subjects of mutual interest, your people will relax, will begin to see you as a normal person – just like them.

The key is to take a wide interest in what is going on around you: read papers, listen to the radio, watch television, and go to the cinema. Make a mental note of what topics interest your people and find out a little more about these. If they say they're going to the football match on Saturday, read up the reports on Sunday. Go and see the sorts of films your people see so that you can discuss them with them. Keep up to date with the soaps, or what's at the top of the charts. You don't have to *like* rap music to *talk* about it.

When people discover that you are genuinely interested in what interests them, then they will become interested in you – and that's when you will have your opportunity to have an informal chat about work, to update them on the latest.

INTEREST FACTORS

- Know which records are in the top 10
- Have an opinion on these records
- Know which films are showing at the local cinema
- Go to see the most popular of these films
- Follow your local football or rugby team (and cricket in the summer)
- Know how other teams are getting on
- Watch TV and establish what your favourite programmes are
- Find out what TV your people watch and watch that, too, occasionally
- Read the occasional tabloid in addition to the highbrow stuff
- Go shopping and find out about new products and special offers
- Try out the local restaurants and have an opinion on them
- Read up on royalty and have an opinion on them
- Have an opinion about the NHS, education, and transportation
- Follow house prices
- Have a story ready to tell about your bank
- Have opinions on various popular holiday destinations
- Know which hotels to recommend for excellent weekend breaks
- Be on the ball when it comes to other people's illnesses, babies, children's progress, marriages, separations, divorces, and bereavements
- Have a smattering of knowledge about gardens and DIY
- Visit the local beauty spots and praise them
- Have an opinion about all types of food (Indian, Mexican, Chinese) as well as all types of alcoholic beverage (but don't drink excessively in pursuing this interest!)

Most people are more centred on their families than they ever are on their work. So, find out about their families. You are on safe ground here because this is their area of real expertise. Find out what's happening to their husbands or wives, to their sons and daughters, to their mothers and fathers. It makes sense when you think about it – families are the most important thing in most people's lives, so it's worth dwelling on the subject whenever you can.

Create opportunities to have a casual chat with your people about what's going on in their lives – what they did at the weekend, what they did last night, what they plan to do next weekend, what holidays they have lined up, what events are taking place in their families.

All this might sound perfectly obvious to many of you, but I get reports of too many bosses who get wrapped up in their own thing, who couldn't tell the difference between one style of pop music and another, who would think Meatloaf was something you ate.

You need to take care, however, in striking up casual conversations with your people. Certain topics are taboo and, if raised, will lead to fierce argument or a high degree of embarrassment. These should be avoided – not because you are not interested, but because there is a high risk of alienation.

TOPICS TO AVOID AT WORK (POTENTIAL TABOOS)

- **Religion**
- **Serious politics (especially if you know the other person has strong views)**
- **Other people's inadequacies**
- **Anything with overtones of inequality (racism, sexism, etc.)**
- **Anything that you know the other person is obsessive about**
- **Anything that you know the other person has very fixed views about**
- **Anything to do with anyone's sex life**
- **Anything that damages another person (reputation, credibility)**

PRINCIPLE:
People are interested in bosses who are interested in them.

PRACTICE:
Just get around and chat to your people and find out what interests them outside work. Then take interest in that yourself.

43

Provide focus

A great boss should be the focus for progress.

It happens to all of us. We drift. We lose perspective. We can't see the wood for the trees (we bark up the wrong tree!) We get confused. We misunderstand. We jump to conclusions. We go off the rails or even get into a rut. We are too easily influenced. We fail to appreciate what it's all about. We don't see the good points, only the bad ones. We exaggerate, distort, manipulate. We allow our hearts to rule our heads. We take it out on other people when we've had a bad time, through no fault of theirs. We expect too much and are disappointed. We don't see the point. We talk too much, don't listen, don't take it all in. We only hear what we want to hear. We turn a blind eye, a deaf ear. We go along with the crowd. We don't think, we get into automatic mode. We become impulsive. We react in a totally unpredictable and often irrational way. We complain too much. We see everything in a bad light. At times, we just don't know what to do, there seems to be no way out. It always seems to be somebody else's fault. We can't see ourselves for what we are. It's always them. We don't know what's going on and feel unloved. We crave gossip and rumour and then believe it's all true. We get things out of proportion. We even become impossible to work with, let alone live with.

Overall, we tend to lose focus on what it's all about. It's there to see in marriages (absence makes the heart grow fonder). It's also there to see at work.

From time to time, people need to be brought back into line. They need to be reminded of the direction they're going in, of how important certain things are, of what the true facts are. They need to

136

sweep the mist from their eyes and see clearly.

They need to be reminded what the business is all about, why their jobs depend on its survival and success, what their real contribution is. They need to know how they fit in and they need a degree of reassurance of how you see their future.

It is very easy to lose sight of the good things in life. That's why holidays are invaluable. You begin to see things in a different light – and that light re-energizes, restores belief and motivation.

The same need is there at work. The best person to provide that focus is the boss. It requires wisdom, tolerance, and perception, as well as the ability to articulate a balanced and helpful view.

How can people appreciate the way their efforts dovetail into the achievement of the organization's longer-term plans unless you bring those plans into focus for them? How will people know they're going off-beam unless you help them refocus on their own

---

FOCAL POINTS

- **Direction of the organization**
- **Direction of the department/section**
- **Giving good service to customers**
- **Money**
- **Innovation and change**
- **Training**
- **Efficiency (equipment, people)**
- **Competitors**
- **People**
- **Our approach (to getting things done)**
- **Sales**
- **External relationships**
- **Plans**
- **Publicity**

direction? How can people value the support of their colleagues unless you bring it into focus and reinforce it? How can people resolve seemingly intractable problems unless you help them focus on options and the creation of solutions that had not previously occurred to them?

It should be clear. When you drive a car you carefully focus on the road ahead because to drift out of focus is incredibly dangerous. People drift out of focus at work. We all do it. We are distracted, we exaggerate thoughts in our minds. A great boss will be aware when this is happening, will detect the blur, and will help people see through it.

It might just mean pulling one or two people together to talk things through, to get all the facts on the table and review them. It might mean the occasional presentation about what's happening in the market-place, or to the competition, or what new directions the top bosses are exploring. It might just mean ensuring that when people comment personally about others that a fair and balanced view is presented.

Focus is essential at work. The great boss provides it continually.

PRINCIPLE:
To reach any destination you must have the way forward clearly in focus.

PRACTICE:
Help your people keep the aim in sight by taking action if you see them drifting off course.

44

Provide a trusted shoulder to lean on

A solid shoulder is the epitome of real trust.

Our understanding of most people is skin-deep. We see the surface and draw our conclusions accordingly. The surface is inevitably an act. In front of their bosses, many play out a role, trying to impress, trying to behave in a way that is consistent with their boss' expectations.

First impressions are rarely right, nor are longer-term ones. It is incredibly difficult to see people as they really are. That is why so many marriages end in divorce. We get deluded with our fantasies of how the person should be, neglecting – until it is too late – the many signals indicating that the real person is far removed from our fantasy image of him or her. The same applies in the workplace. We formulate our impressions of people in simplistic terms, saying that Jenny is 'enthusiastic', Paul is a 'slow learner', Karen is a 'dreamer'.

By putting people into two-dimensional boxes we divorce ourselves from the reality, we close off our minds from understanding the real person. We are in danger of reacting to our simple *image* of the person rather than to the *real* person. Labels don't help either. We react to Jackie in a certain way because she is the trade union official. We would react differently if we saw her simply as a human being, with no stereotypical label attached.

Consequently, our relationships at work are often founded on these superficial impressions.

THE KEYS TO TRUST

- **Finding the time for people**
- **Taking an interest in people**
- **Never making others feel bad**
- **Always trying to help**
- **Listening attentively to others' problems**
- **Ensuring total confidentiality**
- **Avoiding value judgements**

'What I like about my boss is that I can take my problems to her. She is always interested, always tries to help. I know she is very busy but she will find me the time if I need it, and she will never make me feel bad.'

What we often don't know is what goes on beneath the surface. We don't really know what's in a person's mind or how they are really feeling, yet what is below the surface can often have a dramatic impact on a person's effectiveness at work. The risk is that a hidden problem blows up in due course, catching us totally unawares and presenting us with a far greater problem than is necessary.

To get below the surface and catch the problem early, we have to develop trust. Trust is too easily eroded! As soon as we let others down, by betraying a confidence, by saying one thing and doing another, by abusing the system, then trust is eroded. Trust can only be built through establishing total reliability and confidentiality as well as total honesty.

Trust, therefore, is of the essence to achieving superb relationships at work.

You must make it very clear, therefore, that you will never let your people down and also that you trust them implicitly. Furthermore, you must make it clear that you will be very unhappy if there is any erosion of that trust. By reinforcing this mutual trust, your people will be confident that they can talk to you about their problems, knowing that such exposure will not backfire on them when it comes to reviewing salaries or making decisions about promotion.

By maintaining a climate of trust, your people will feel they can turn to you for advice and help on any matter, whether it be personal or work-related. They will value your support and the simple fact that you are prepared to give them time, that you can listen and understand. However, providing a shoulder to lean on does not mean automatically offering solutions to everyone's problems. Most people, by talking through their problems with someone they trust, will find their own solutions.

We all experience problems from time to time. In talking them through with another we expose our vulnerabilities, our desperations, our frustrations. We therefore have to trust that this person will not exploit what we perceive as our own weaknesses.

By providing a shoulder to lean on, a great boss will help a person get things into perspective, will help that person see things clearly, will encourage that person to pursue a positive direction to resolve the problem. It will be a cathartic experience, enabling someone to purge themselves of the distortions, complexities, and uncertainties in their thinking and feelings. In doing so, the process will be of great value, not only to the person but also to the organization as a whole.

It is fashionable to say that one of the roles of a modern manager is to act as a counsellor, or coach, or supporter. Essentially, though, it is all down to a simple common-sense fact – that to manage effectively you have to enjoy good relationships with your people, and to enjoy good relationships you have to have a high degree of mutual trust. One way of demonstrating that is to provide a reliable shoulder to lean on.

PRINCIPLE:
People only turn to those they trust for help.

PRACTICE:
Never make value judgements when people expose their thoughts and feelings to you.

Always listen carefully when people bring their problems to you. Try to understand. Try to guide them through a thought process that leads them to their own solution.

45

Plan with your people

To get from A to B you have to take your people with you. It is critical, therefore, that you involve them in planning how to get there.

Planning is an essential task for any boss. Too many managers allow themselves to get into a routine of merely reacting to events or to demands from their own bosses. They seem to have no clear idea of where they want to take the unit, section, or department. In other words, they have no sense of purpose, no sense of direction.

As mentioned in a previous section, a great boss must know where he (or she) is going. Planning is essential for clarifying the best method for getting there. Furthermore, it is essential to involve your people with this, especially as you need their support in achieving your aims.

Throughout this book it has been stressed that while a boss is accountable for what is achieved, deciding how it is achieved should be left to the people working for that boss – providing certain common-sense boundaries are maintained. Planning is the process of defining what has to be achieved over the next year or two and how it is to be achieved.

Without plans, bosses lose direction, drift off course, confuse their people. A plan, therefore, is vital to the success of any department or section as it actually defines that future success and the means by which a group of people are going to get there.

The process of planning should hold no mystique for any boss. It is not as complicated as many think. Again, it is based on asking and answering certain common-sense questions about the business and the way forward. To achieve any credibility, the plan must quantify certain dimensions of the business. Thus, there should be a quantification of the units of production or service to be produced by the department or section as well as the costs involved. Many service managers struggle with this, possibly knowing full well what their costs are but having no idea how to quantify what they deliver to their customers (internal or external). This applies especially to central departments. However, a failure to measure output will make it exceptionally difficult to justify your existence, because there is no real measure of what value you add to the organization. That is why so many organizations nowadays are splitting into smaller autonomous business units that trade internally with each other.

To begin the planning process, you should aim to take those people who report to you away for a couple of days to a pleasant hotel in order to review where you are currently, where you want to be in a year or two year's time, and how you're going to get there. In some industries, you need to plan up to five years ahead (or even more), but, in some cases, one to two years is adequate. The world is rapidly changing and there are always unforeseen events, so it is likely that your plan is going to have to be revised within a year in any case.

THE PLAN

1   What business are we in?
2   What products/services does our unit supply?
3   What is our track record?
4   Who are our customers (internal or external)?
5   Who are our competitors?
6   What makes our business unique?
7   Let's visualize our long-term future success: what does it look like (in terms of customers, market, product, operations, organization, people, systems, finance)?
8   What are our main goals for the future?
9   Let's quantify these goals (e.g. in terms of units of production/ service, market share, sales revenue, etc.)
10   Let's quantify the costs involved in achieving our future goals.
11   What steps do we need to take over the next year to achieve our goals?
12   What immediate actions do we need to take?

Having spent a couple of days thrashing out your long-term goals and the steps needed to get there, you now need to go back to the office to develop your ideas and produce a first draft plan. It is critical that this first draft is tested to the point of destruction. Every word and every figure in the plan should be able to withstand challenge.

By getting your people involved in the process of producing a plan, you secure their commitment. This will add credibility to the plan and give power to your elbow when you are seeking approval for it. Furthermore, by involving your people you are likely to produce a far better plan than if you had attempted it by yourself.

It is always wise to have your people with you when you present your plan to your own boss. They will be able to support you and answer difficult questions that fox you.

The finished plan, ideally, should be a high-quality presentation neatly bound with a desk-top published production. This will give your people pride in it and also assist in getting approval.

Remember that the plan is all about securing your future jobs, your future successes, your future as a department or section, as you see it.

PRINCIPLE:
The best way to get from A to B is to have a plan for getting there.

PRACTICE:
Work closely with your people to clarify where you want to get to and the best way to get there.

46
Keep your distance

Never too close, never too far away.

One of the most difficult lines to draw at work is between people you like and those you don't. It is even worse when you're the boss. The problem of favouritism has been dealt with in a previous section, but the issue here is how close should you get to your people, whether they be favourites or not. If you stand too far away from them, you will be accused of being aloof and distant; if you get too close, you will be seen as 'one of the boys' (or girls) and will risk losing respect.

Also covered in a previous section is the critical importance of taking an interest in your people. The question here is the *extent* to which you should limit that interest. Every person you know will have an invisible boundary around himself (or herself) within which you should not stray. It is a boundary of privacy, of inner thoughts and feelings that people are reluctant to reveal except to their closest confidants. It is unlikely that, as the boss, you should be that confidant, but if you were it is questionable whether you should be. Unless you have the professional skills of a counsellor, there is always a high risk that you become emotionally involved with a person you are trying to help. The dangers are obvious. While it is important that you provide a trusted shoulder to lean on, that support should never extend into areas of intimate revelation. The skill is to recognize the boundary and not step over it.

Emotional attachments between a boss and one of his or her people can be potentially destructive. Ideally, such relationships should be avoided, but if they do occur, they must be kept outside the workplace. If conducted at work, they will prove divisive and have a negative impact on everyone around.

The problem is a surreptitious one. We gravitate towards people we like. There is an equally strong pull towards people who like us. We spend more time with these people and learn more about them than we do about people we like less. That learning brings us closer together. Without due care, we can suddenly find that the invisible boundary between ourselves and a subordinate has disappeared and that we are wallowing in each other's emotional confusions.

Learn to recognize the danger signs. Learn to step back when you begin to say to yourself, 'I want to spend more time with this person'. Don't delude yourself that your desire to be with this person is purely for professional purposes, or for welfare reasons, or totally objective, albeit supportive.

As you approach that all-important boundary of personal intimacy, think carefully through the consequences of breaching it. Once crossed, matters can soon get out of hand and you will struggle to keep control. As a boss, you *must* be in control, especially of yourself.

There are other dangers, too, of getting too close to people at work. Personal confidences can be leaked and rebound on you. Furthermore, by stepping across that boundary, people will get the impression that you will be on their side when a difficult decision has to be made. They will feel betrayed if your decisions then go against them. It is exemplified by the quandary 'Could you sack your best friend?'

Becoming a great boss is not about being in a popularity contest. Occasionally decisions have to be made that, no matter how hard you have tried, people don't like. If you are a close friend of a person adversely affected by that decision, it becomes much more difficult to implement it.

In essence, you should not pursue close friendships with the people you manage, or the people who manage you. Such friendships are fraught with danger. Objectivity is lost, and intense emotions enter the fray.

When you go to see a doctor about an intimate and potentially embarrassing medical ailment, you expect the doctor to take a close professional interest – but only in the ailment. As a professional, the doctor will show no emotion towards you as a person. As a

146

manager, you should be similarly professional and should also remain objective in all your dealings with people. This doesn't mean to say that you shouldn't act like a human being by expressing your opinions, views, and non-intimate emotions, but, if there is a danger that such expression can be misinterpreted, or be seen as stepping over the line, then you should hold back.

It is all to do with sensitivity and trust between people at work. It is also about knowing your own personal motivations, and being honest with yourself. To a certain degree, you have to be selfless as a boss, suppressing your own personal desires for affiliation with people you like, for becoming popular, for being 'one of the boys' (or girls). It's a sacrifice you have to make.

Consequently, tread warily when near people you really like. Continually question your own motives. Take the difficult route, avoid close and intimate contact with these people. Never create opportunities to see more of them than others and be careful of their approaches, too. When it comes to love and war, we are all exceptionally good at scheming!

At work, as a boss, you are not involved in love or war.

SCANDAL AND GOSSIP

People love scandals. It's gossip that often keeps them going.

Any personal relationship you allow to develop at work will soon become the centre of a scandal and much gossip. It will be fun for everyone to talk about, but not for you.

The gossip will damage you. The respect people have for you will be diminished. Most importantly, it will impair your chances of reaching the goals you are paid to achieve.

PRINCIPLE:
Close personal contact with your people at work can be highly counter-productive.

PRACTICE:
When dealing with personal issues at work, stop and think, 'Am I stepping over the line?'

47

Take holidays

***If you really want to enjoy your work, make
sure you enjoy regular holidays.***

The importance of getting away from your people to give them a
chance to prove themselves is covered in a later section, but taking
holidays is an essential part of that process. Too many executives
take a perverse pride in working excessive hours, deluding
themselves and others that they are incredibly important, incredibly
busy, and so indispensable that the organization cannot spare them
for an hour, let alone two weeks, or more, in the summer. These are
the same executives who dash off to Paris or Frankfurt to attend
meetings that, in the eyes of everyone but themselves, are non-
essential.

Work should be fun, so there is no harm in putting in extra hours,
especially if you are enjoying yourself and welcome the exhilaration
of meeting exceptionally difficult challenges. What you have to do,
though, as an effective boss, is to question the value of those extra
hours. Too often, extra hours are put in for the sake of appearances,
or as an escape from problems at home, or simply because a boss is
getting too immersed in detail. Also, even if the extra hours are for a
good reason, there is a limit to what you can put in. The risk of
executive burnout is always there.

So, here is a recommendation. Take one long holiday (between two
and three weeks) each year. Furthermore, take three short holidays
each year (two or three days tacked on to a weekend).

Create fantasies in your mind about these holidays. Create a picture
of an idyllic two weeks where you get away from it all and really
indulge yourself in what you want to do. It could be a couple of

weeks in Cyprus, or 'munro' walking in Scotland, or a trip to Florida for your third visit to see Universal Studios, or pottering around Devon and Cornwall. You might even visit Thailand. Conjure up exactly what you would like to do on this holiday, whether it be relaxing with a cappuccino in a harbour-side café, watching the world go by, sunbathing on a white sandy beach, or seeing the sights in Rome or Paris or Disney World.

Having fixed the fantasy in your mind, move towards it. Go and collect a few brochures from your local travel agent and spend an enjoyable evening with your family reviewing the various options. Converge on a decision and book the holiday.

All this is excellent practice for what you should really be doing at work. It is important to create pictures in your mind (visions) of what you want to achieve. It is very important to involve your people in the process. It is very important to ensure that decisions are made and implemented.

THE ADVANTAGES OF HOLIDAYS

- **Recharging batteries (regenerating enthusiasm)**
- **Gaining perspective (seeing things differently)**
- **Rebalancing priorities (re-establishing what's important to you)**
- **Spending time with your family**
- **Removing tension pains, relieving stress**
- **Finding new energies**
- **Learning from non-routine situations (observing other people on holiday, meeting totally different people, absorbing different cultures)**
- **Creating new ideas**
- **Getting fitter**
- **Catching up on your reading (anything but work-related books)**
- **Indulging yourself for a while (good food, good wine, etc.)**
- **Reinforcing your awareness that there is more to life than work**

By taking holidays you become a human being again. You relearn the art and skill of sending postcards, of buying ice-creams, and applying suntan lotion to your partner's back. By dressing in casual clothes, you suddenly become ordinary in the eyes of others. You get lost in the crowd. You cease to be important.

Furthermore, holidays provide a range of useful conversation topics for that all-important small talk (everyone is an expert on holidays and has a view to debate with you).

When you get back from holiday you will find that you are a thousand times more effective than when you went away. However, the effect wears off after a short while and you will need to be planning to go away again in two or three months' time.

Your task today is to book your holiday (if you haven't done so already). If you have done so, get your diary out and blank out the days for 3 or 4 breaks over the next 12 months.

PRINCIPLE:
Holidays are essential to sustaining effectiveness at work.

PRACTICE:
Plan one year ahead by scheduling at least one long holiday and three or four short ones.

Always have one holiday booked in advance.

48

Fire every thousandth employee

One in a thousand people are impossible. Don't hire them. If you do. Fire them.

Well, not exactly one in a thousand! Take this with a pinch of salt. However, the world is not so perfect that every single person you manage is motivated, is going to produce fine work, or even has the potential to do so as a result of your nurturing.

Very rarely, you are going to come across a real dud. Somebody who, despite all your efforts, fails to achieve a tenth of what you could reasonably expect. The best thing about them might be their smile, the worst thing the quality and quantity of their work.

I am afraid that in this harsh old world, there is a limited place for charity in business. You cannot afford to be charitable towards people who continually fail to deliver, whatever the reason. You have to admit your mistakes and fire the poor performers before they cause irreparable damage.

Furthermore, your people will see the problem before you do, and they will expect you to act. They will expect you to fire the odd person. Your credibility will be severely damaged if you ignore poor performers and fail to face up to them. Your people should be proud of what they do and can accomplish. They will not want any misfit to drag them down.

You have to face up to the statistical probability that you will not go through your life as a boss without coming across a person you have to sack. You don't need to go searching, it will become glaringly obvious to you that this particular person is not making it, and never will. The risk is that this person will consume a vast amount of your time (and that of your people) in bailing him or her out of difficult situations.

So, take action! But also take care! The decision is important but equally so is the way you approach it and the way you implement it. Care is of the essence. Care means the application of sensitivity, fairness, understanding, and help to the person being fired.

It is easy to forget that the person you are firing is a human being. The process will be traumatic, for him (or her) and you. Back home, there will probably be a family to face, neighbours to talk to, friends in the pub or club. The reasons you give for your action will rarely be the reasons given to the family, neighbours, or friends – 'Things didn't work out', 'My face didn't fit', 'I couldn't get on with my boss', 'I didn't like the work'. Face-saving will be the order of the day and no matter how open and honest you are, you will have to collude with this to a degree. Don't be dishonest, but find words that help.

Ideally (and this is your target) you should aim to persuade people you have to fire that it is the best thing that could happen to them. Great bosses achieve this. They help the person realize that the lack of results, the poor quality of work was all due to a lack of suitability of the job, which inevitably leads to a lack of satisfaction. In other words, sacking a person can often be in that person's best interests – creating opportunities elsewhere which were not available in the current job and therefore were not exploiting that person's real talents (we all have talents).

The decision to fire someone is a big one and there's always a danger that a mistake is made. To avoid this and as part of the caring process, it is important to give an early warning of the possibility of dismissal. Most organizations have clearly laid out procedures for this – in fact, the law requires it. As a boss, therefore, you have to be scrupulously fair and totally objective in pursuing a potential termination to prevent accusations of unfair dismissal. You should ensure that minor incidents, minor failures and temporary aberrations are not exaggerated out of all proportion to justify any personal grudge you have against a person. In other words, no personal prejudice should ever enter the reasoning process. Likes and dislikes are irrelevant when it comes to firing people.

THREE REASONS

There can only be three reasons for firing an employee:

1 there are *substantial* deficiencies (in the quantity and/or quality of someone's work) that continue over a period of time despite warnings and despite every conceivable effort having been made to help this person eliminate these deficiencies.
2 the person's conduct is grossly unacceptable (thieving, harassment, intimidation, violence, etc.)
3 redundancy (the job ceases to exist).

Fortunately, the larger part of your efforts as a boss will be concentrated on the 99.9 per cent of people who perform effectively and have the potential to contribute even more. However, when you come across the impossible person you will find that a vast amount of your time is consumed by this person and that firing is the only answer to what otherwise would be an intractable problem.

Never risk keeping these people on. The damage can be too great.

PRINCIPLE:
Never accept continuing poor performance or gross misconduct. Fire persistent offenders.

Deal with such deficiencies in a caring way. Fire fairly.

PRACTICE:
Be scrupulous in pursuing the correct procedures for firing a person. Even so, do not shy away from such a decision.

49

Learn the language

If you don't know what they're talking about, your credibility will suffer.

There is a lot of confusion about the role of a manager and whether they should possess a degree of technical expertise in the area of the people working for them.

A critical factor in the success of any manager is personal relationships and this is largely to do with communications, understandings, and commitments. None of this can be achieved if you don't understand what your people are doing and don't know what they are talking about. That doesn't mean that you have to be as expert as they are. Most people can understand what a car mechanic does without being able to repair a car.

Most bosses come up through professional routes such as accountancy, sales, or engineering. The worst of them continue to practise their professions on becoming managers, continuing to play with financial figures, or continuing to sell, or continuing to pore over engineering designs. It's their profession that gives them the buzz, not managing people. There are other ineffective bosses who have no idea of what's going on, who don't understand the figures, who have no idea about selling, or who shy away from anything technical.

The middle road is the best road. You should learn something of the trade, but, as a manager, never attempt to practise it. An appreciation and understanding of the skills of your people and the intricacies of their trade will enable you to relate their contribution to the organization's overall goals.

Too many professionals like to create a mystical aura about their expertise, barring outsiders from intruding on their sacred territory of special knowledge. The medical profession used to excel at this, treating patients as naive, ignorant people who would endanger themselves if they dared to ask other than simple questions about what was happening to their bodies. Even today I have come across doctors who prefer to tell me that my blood pressure is 'OK' rather than inform me that it's 130/80 with a pulse of 60 and explain what this means. Mercifully, most doctors are changing.

The weak bosses allow their people to shower them with technical jargon. The best bosses probe a little further and find out what this jargon means. Often it's not difficult. After all, you don't need an accountancy qualification to be able to read a balance sheet.

The challenge before you is to learn the language of the various professional groups for which you are responsible. Never attempt to do their jobs *for* them, but do attempt to *understand* their jobs. Don't be frightened to ask seemingly naive questions. Most professionals, not all, will realize that you don't know the language and will be only too pleased to explain what they mean by a TCA, RGI, or PRPS.

In some cases, the technical experts will even allow you, as the boss, to undertake some of the simple tasks of their trade. Then you'll find how difficult their job really is. It will help you appreciate the years of experience and training that has gone in to making them so skilled at what they do.

LANGUAGE

Learn the meaning of:

- **commonly used technical terms (bytes)**
- **commonly used professional terms (margin, contribution)**
- **acronyms (LGR, CCT)**
- **local idiom (the Portakabin crew)**
- **management terms (focus groups)**
- **organization language (divisions, departments, sections)**

Take the organization's documentation home, the reports, the professional journals and study them, highlighting words and terms you don't understand. Then go in the next day and find out what they mean.

The more conversant you become in the language of the people you are working with, the more likely you are to strike up effective and meaningful relationships with them. In doing so, the traditional gap between managers and workers will be closed and you will be more able to work together to achieve the organization's goals.

PRINCIPLE:
To relate to people you have to understand their language.

PRACTICE:
If you don't understand what people are saying, always find out, never let it pass by.

Make a conscious effort to learn the language of your people.

50

Admit your mistakes

The power of honesty lies in the admission of what you do wrong, not in what you do right.

Mistakes are much more interesting than things done right, so make your life interesting, look at your own mistakes.

Other people's mistakes are also fascinating and can provide valuable lessons. So, study successful people and find out how they benefited from their mistakes. Even your heroes and heroines are not that perfect.

The problem with mistakes is that they are difficult to define and, therefore, difficult to admit and learn from. Knocking over a cup of coffee is easy, so is getting your boss' wife's or husband's name wrong. Similarly, forgetting to attend a meeting or failing to send an enclosure with a letter can easily be done.

However, there are many other mistakes that fox us. How do we know when we've hired the wrong person? How do we know we're in the wrong job? How do we know we handled that situation badly? How do we know we've inadvertently offended someone?

It is quite clear when other people make mistakes. Faulting others' behaviour is a popular pastime. We talk about it all the time. For example, we complain to our close friends when someone makes us feel small, ignores us, shouts at us, distorts things, deceives us, lets us down, or generally makes us feel bad. The problem is that the offenders we complain about rarely realize they're making the mistakes we accuse them of behind their backs.

Perception, or perhaps lack of perception, therefore plays a vital role in accepting and admitting mistakes. Our perceptions of mistakes relate to the degree of conformance to our own and other people's standards. Knocking over a cup of coffee does not conform to anyone's standard so we will freely admit the mistake (though a few people will blame another for putting the cup on the edge of the table).

It is when standards diverge that we encounter the biggest problems over admitting mistakes. It is also when we are unaware of our own behaviours and actions and how they deviate from accepted standards. It is all too easy to allow our standards to drop to the lowest common denominator. Bad behaviour can become the norm (everyone drops litter, everyone swears, everyone fiddles their expenses). We no longer see our own weaknesses and failings, we become divorced from the accepted standards, allowing our own impulses to drive us and forever claiming the righteousness of our ways. We end up by failing to see ourselves for what we are. We discourage feedback for fear of being exposed. We hate the pain of such exposure, denying the truth. We don't like to be told we are fat, that we made a mistake in eating all those terrible things. We close our minds to the bad news and delude ourselves by allowing only good news to filter in.

We create an image of ourselves that is totally unrelated to reality. The image distorts the interpretation of our own behaviours. Our own behaviours deteriorate and, as a consequence, we make mistakes in the eyes of everyone but ourselves.

Admitting mistakes, therefore, is not simply a matter of piecemeal confessions for the mishaps we make in our lives. It is more a matter of looking at ourselves and understanding our own deep-rooted defects. We all have them. Many defects cannot be corrected, but at least awareness of them will enable us to neutralize the defect so that it does not cause damage. If you can't spell, don't make the mistake of getting a job requiring a lot of writing. If you can't make presentations, don't make the mistake of becoming a trainer. If you like to be popular, don't make the mistake of becoming a manager!

A high degree of self-awareness minimizes the possibility of making mistakes. Such self-awareness gives strength and leads to self-belief. When you have a high degree of self-awareness and self-belief, you more readily admit your mistakes, you more readily learn the lessons, and that's when you become stronger in your pursuits. As a result, you are more likely to be successful.

Such strength enables you to face up to other people, to go to your boss and the people you work with and admit you've done something wrong.

When there's been a screw-up many people will, like wolves, bay for blood. They will hunt for the culprit. If it's you and you own up, the baying and the hunting will stop. Suddenly the wolves will become human. They will side with you – 'There, but for the grace of God ...'.

Honesty pays. Admitting mistakes is all about honesty. Honesty is all about revealing deeper truths about yourself.

For such revelation you need people around you who can be completely honest with you. These are people who are fearless in telling you how they see you: your behaviour, your actions, your decisions, your words. Such revelation is suppressed in a traditional hierarchical organization, and that's why so many of them are crumbling.

You can only admit mistakes to people you trust. Those you don't will exploit your mistakes to their own ends. Conversely, never exploit another person's mistake, rather, learn from it – you will both benefit.

Trust your people and admit your mistakes to them. They will respect you more than if you try to cover up or cast blame elsewhere.

PRINCIPLE:
Total honesty and self-awareness about your own shortcomings.

PRACTICE:
Get people to tell you when you fail.
Challenge yourself continually about what you do right, and what you do wrong.

51

Take the initiative

Always be the first to make a positive move (especially when others hesitate).

Taking initiatives is all about thinking for yourself. If you follow the rule book slavishly, if you follow others or even wait for others you will lose time and lose the initiative.

It means getting there first, being the first to volunteer for a difficult assignment, the first to speak up, the first to challenge an ill-conceived idea.

It means getting to the customer first, too. The worst thing that can happen is having the *customer* tell *you* that there is a problem. Taking the initiative means advising the customer of a late delivery *before* they advise you.

It means getting to your people first, too, especially with vital information. To be credible as a boss, you have to beat the grapevine.

Too many bosses stick their head in the sand and wait for the problem to go away – the intractable problems about car-parking spaces, company cars, and office accommodation. Fix the problem now, or at least within the next four weeks

There is a saying that if you think about it too long you'll never get it done. Some bosses just get it done. They take the initiative and do it. The problem with large bureaucratic organizations is that everyone waits for each other to agree. Working parties, steering committees and focus groups are set up to review the problem and make recommendations that then have to be 'sold' to others who have not been involved and who then proceed to pick holes in the solutions proposed. Thousands of hours are wasted as people sit around in meetings arguing about the best way forward. The danger is that you end up with the lowest common denominator – and that's bad for customers, bad for employees, and, ultimately, bad for the business.

Taking the initiative means seizing accountability. It means taking risks by taking the burden of a decision on your own shoulders. It means cutting through the red tape and authorizing the expenditure, knowing that others might not only disagree but disapprove. It means getting results, and, occasionally, making mistakes.

Taking the initiative means seizing opportunities. Opportunities fly by at a phenomenal speed. If you wait for a committee to decide, the opportunity will have flown out of the window and been snatched up by a competitor.

Taking the initiative means concentrating on doing little things to please your customers as well as your people. They might seem little to you but to the people who benefit from them they will appear very important. It is taking the initiative to send people 'Thank you' cards, to call them up and show an interest when they least expect it, to pop in and see someone on your travels, to get one of your more junior people to do the overseas trip on your behalf.

Taking the initiative is about pursuing really exciting ideas, experimenting with new products and services, bringing in new technology before others do. It means going out and finding the best training for your people, ensuring that they are exposed to the latest thinking before it becomes commonplace. It means finding time for the simple courtesies and everyday basics of working life; like walking around to have a chat and finding out what's going on, like saying 'Hello' and asking after the kids. It means following up on things that were raised with you last time you walked around.

As a boss, you should not be the sole custodian of initiative. Welcome positive action taken by your people. Support and encourage such initiative. Too many bosses inwardly resent such initiative, taking it as a slight for not having thought of it themselves. They pour cold water on ideas initiated by their people, seeing such initiative as implied criticism. If your people get there first, rejoice! Congratulate them for being ahead of you. And the same with your own boss. Don't react as if they are treading on your toes, invading your patch, or making a move that you should have thought of but didn't.

Sit back today and reflect on the initiatives (no mater how small) you and your people have taken over the last three months. Assess the positive impact these initiatives have had on the business.

Aim to develop a group of people with a reputation for initiative, who are streets ahead of the rest of the organization and, more importantly, of the competition. Take pride in getting there first, in seizing opportunities, in cracking problems that others find intractable.

PRINCIPLE:
Seizing opportunities to be ahead of the competition.

PRACTICE:
Hesitate before saying 'no' or 'it can't be done'.

Spend less time thinking and talking about how to crack problems and more time taking real action to overcome them.

Discipline yourself to look out for opportunities and to seize them.

Take risks and do not be fearful of them.

52

Put your job on the line

There are certain occasions in life when the courage of your convictions will be tested by having to put your job on the line.

Disagreement should be a healthy, everyday aspect of working life. It is through disagreement and discussion that better decisions are reached. However, there are certain fundamental issues in life on which it is impossible to agree with the other person. These normally relate to deeply held principles and beliefs.

Ideally, such major disagreements should not happen at all; in practice, they happen rarely. They should not happen because we tend to join organizations that we think demonstrate the same values and beliefs as we hold, that already employ like-minded people we instinctively know we can work with, that offer work we will find interesting and can subscribe wholeheartedly to. In other words, an effective recruitment process should flush out those dissenters who do not passionately support the cause of the organization, who will not work in harmony with their colleagues and their bosses.

Inevitably, this ideal state is not always achieved and, frequently, an organization breeds a group of dissenters who stir up trouble and indirectly drag the organization down.

The danger is that you, as a boss, get sucked into this dissent and allow yourself to frequently bad-mouth your own bosses and the organization as a whole. Such behaviour will be a reflection of your own inadequacies and your lack of courage in tackling difficult issues or tolerating things you don't like. It will indicate to the people around you that you have no moral fibre, no backbone, and are prepared to sink to the same depths as the rabble of moaners and groaners, cynics and whingers who infect many large organizations.

When you have a major disagreement with the way the organization is being run, or with an important decision that is being made, or the way your boss is behaving, you must first confront the appropriate person. Normally this would be your own boss. You must create an opportunity to see your boss and express your views and your feelings on the issue in question. You must explain that you fundamentally disagree with the way the organization (or the boss) is running things and that it goes completely against your own principles and beliefs. In other words, you must attempt to persuade your boss of your conviction that certain practices and decisions are unacceptable to you. It is only fair then that you give your boss or your employer an opportunity to respond and attempt to convince you about the way they are going about things. They might even be persuaded by your own argument and agree to change. Should agreement not be reached and there is a failure to resolve the problem, you have two options, and these are outlined below.

FUNDAMENTAL DISAGREEMENTS: THE TWO OPTIONS

Option 1

Having talked things through, you forget your disagreement, you defer to your boss or the organization, and you willingly cooperate.

Option 2

You resign.

The forbidden option

To continue moaning and groaning about decisions and the way things are being run.

You should only put your job on the line when, in all conscience, you can no longer live with what's going on. This will happen when you are forced to cooperate with bad practices, or when your health is threatened by doing things against your better judgement. It will happen when you are asked to go against your conscience.

Before taking such a bold step, it is important to thrash out the implications with your husband, wife, or partner at home. The risk is that by tomorrow you will be out of a job, that your family's livelihood will be substantially affected. You must examine your own views carefully. Are you getting things out of proportion? Is it that you are not seeing things straight? Are you absolutely sure you are right about this issue? Is it really a matter of conviction? Do you have the courage to pursue the issue all the way through? What happens if your boss calls your bluff, will you resign?

You should only resign if you can neither live with what's going on nor change it. Many people who have been through the trauma of resigning on principle will say that it's the best thing that ever happened to them. They created new careers elsewhere that allowed them to exploit those talents that had been suppressed by the employer they had rebelled against.

Whichever route you choose, you need to do an immense amount of clear thinking. It's a decision you should not take lightly, nor too frequently, but it's a decision you should take if the organization is going against fundamental principles you hold.

PRINCIPLE:
Having the courage of your convictions.

PRACTICE:
Resign if the organization goes against certain of your deeply held convictions.

53

Be human

Too many bosses act out the role and, in doing so, lose their humanity.

We all tend to build up images about people and then react to the images, not the people. Frequently these images are distorted or based on prejudice. Rarely are they formed through objective analysis and rational construction. These images are stereotypes. We expect certain types of people to behave in a certain type of way. For example, politicians. We form images of politicians: 'They never listen, they never answer a question directly, they are full of their own dogma and rhetoric. They toe the party line. They have the gift of the gab'. That is our image. So, when we hear and see politicians, we filter out information that conflicts with our image of them and select only that which reinforces our view.

Regrettably, too many people assimilate the image others have of them and cease to be themselves. They act out the role others expect of them. The headteacher ceases to be a human being but simulates a role that is consistent with our image of a headteacher. As a result, we lose sight of the real person. Our behaviours reflect off the images we have of each other rather than express the reality of our true selves.

In a hierarchy, this can be incredibly dangerous. We create a 'boss' image and behave accordingly - deferring to status, accepting decisions without question. In a hierarchy, we are eager to please, even if we are not pleased. We hide our true thoughts and feelings, we acquiesce, we manipulate, we distort, we present the surface - the superficial smile, the illusion of hard work. Reality is suppressed as we play with the images we have of each other.

Image creation is an industry and undoubtedly necessary when trying to distil the essence of a product, service (or even person) to a wide public. Even so, the best image is one that is consistent with the reality. Image creation is of no use when attempting to develop excellent one-to-one relationships. The more you get to know a person, the more you see through the image that person sought to create in your mind in the first place. If that person persists in maintaining an image divorced from the perceptions of others, then relationship problems will inevitably occur.

As a boss the key is not to attempt to create an image of how you *think* a boss should be, or of how you think your people think a boss should be: the key is to be human. That means sweeping away all your preconceptions about certain types of people. It means treating every single person you meet as an equal. It is imperative, therefore, that you forget the labels others attach to people – 'He's a typical personnel man', 'She's a typical accountant'. Equally important, we should resist classifying people into these groups. The groupings become too neat and it's all too easy to make judgements based on prejudicial assumptions about how these groups behave rather than on their actual behaviour or reasons for it. The way we react to fame is a good example. We tend to forget that famous people are humans and treat them like demi-gods. Conversely, some famous people lose touch with humanity and become inhuman. The way we treat royalty and they treat us is another example.

Bosses can be like royals. They become self-important and create an image that reinforces this. They become self-righteous. They cease to be humble, they lose their respect for others who are not bosses. Their self-importance effectively devalues the contribution of front-line people who are not accorded the same privileges.

I've had some great bosses in my time. The way for them appeared easy and was based on common sense. They treated me like a real person, an equal. They trusted me, respected me, listened to me. They confided in me, joked with me. They took a genuine interest in me. They even expected a lot of me – and I gave it, and they appreciated it.

It's simple really. It's common sense again. To get the best out of people you have to treat them like human beings.

MORE CLICHÉS

- 'Treat a man like a dog and he'll behave like a dog'
- 'Pay peanuts, get monkeys'
- 'Beauty is in the eye of the beholder'
- 'The Emperor wears no clothes'
- 'Take people at face value'

We all start off with the same number of legs, arms, eyes, and ears. Then, society conditions us to believe we are different. Middle class, upper class, rich, poor, Southerner, Northerner, and so on. We are, of course, different, but the key is to create our own difference rather than be conditioned to conform to one of the established stereotypes. If I were a trade union official, for example, it would be all too easy to conform to the stereotype for this role - that is, to make life difficult for management.

The essence of humanity is to establish our own individual uniqueness and express it. At the same time, we need to recognize the uniqueness of others and welcome their expression of it.

To be a great boss is to be human and to demonstrate it.

PRINCIPLE:
Treating everyone as human beings and equally.

PRACTICE:
Resist stereotyping people in your own mind and also resist reacting to this stereotype.

Take an equal interest in everyone.

Don't make assumptions about people just because of their status or position in the organization.

Take people at face value.

54

Hire the best people

Find the best, keep the best, be the best.

Many companies fail at this first hurdle. They are expedient, taking the first, paying the least, not looking twice. They go for short-term gain, fearful to delay things by seeking out the best.

To be really successful as a boss, you must invest heavily in hiring the best people. This calls for an inordinate amount of time, energy, and resource. The dividends will be great. Expressed another way, there is no short cut to the recruitment process – rush at it and you will hire the wrong people.

Take care when dabbling in modern techniques, such as psychometric tests, graphology, assessment centres, and other seemingly objective means of assessment. First impressions might well be deceptive. Just look at the giant corporations crashing all around you! They used the latest scientific techniques to hire what they thought were first-rate people.

Recruitment is a high-risk business. Whoever you hire will present a risk to the business, but you have to take that risk. You cannot afford to be cautious by only bringing on board solid citizens who are so sound and secure that they have no imagination for the cut and thrust of modern-day business and, consequently, fail to venture out against the competition.

Spend as much time as possible with each candidate, try to get to know what they're made of, what they really excel at, what switches them on. Skills are relatively easy to develop, and knowledge, too, is easy to acquire. More difficult is changing someone's attitudes. So, go for people with positive attitudes, personalities that are bright, people who can relate to you and your colleagues. Also, go for honesty and courage. Experience counts, but, first and foremost, is the desire to succeed. That should be evident from track records and the way candidates present themselves at interviews.

Don't rely on the first interview. It is a well-worn saying, but very apt; first impressions can be very deceptive. Bring back the short-listed candidates for a day at your location. Show them around and observe their level of interest. Ask them lots of questions. Get them to tell you about their achievements. Invite them to make presentations. In the end, you will know which candidate is the best, which one stands out head and shoulders above the rest.

However, don't just rely on your *own* judgement. The more people you involve in assessing the short-listed candidates, the better your decision will be. Get your people to take the candidates to lunch and then show them around. It is equally critical to involve your boss, too. The chosen person will have to convince everyone, not just you. Listen carefully to the advice proffered by your people, your colleagues, and your boss about each candidate.

THE BEST FOR THE JOB

- **Ensure that you are 100 per cent clear about what you mean by the best**
- **Use the best personnel people (internally) to recruit the best for you (people who really understand what you want)**
- **Otherwise, use the best (external) selection consultants**
- **Go for the best people in the market-place (aim your recruitment advertisements at the best)**
- **Move fast**
- **Ensure your remuneration package is the best**
- **Make sure the person you are recruiting really feels wanted**
- **Provide the very best training**
- **Once on board, give your recruits the best opportunity to demonstrate their talents**
- **Nurture the best**

The most progressive organizations allow people to select their own bosses. That seems quite sensible to me. Do otherwise and you demonstrate your lack of trust. Let your people choose and then endorse their decision.

However, it should be a cardinal rule of recruitment that the person to whom the new recruit reports should make the final selection decision. In other words, never allow other people to make selection decisions for you. You are held accountable for your business results, so you must be held accountable for choosing who should be working for you. You can let your people help you decide, but, in the end, it is still your decision.

Finding the best people to join your group is perhaps one of the biggest challenges you will face. Make the right decision and you will have few problems in the long term. The best people make it relatively easy for you. They also make it easy for your customers. Why inflict other than the best people on your customers? You find second-best people everywhere at the customer interface – people who don't smile, who never take initiatives, who have no idea at all. The result is a second-rate service.

In other words, to achieve the very best for your customers, you cannot afford to do other than hire the best people to serve them.

PRINCIPLE:
The best people generate the best results.

PRACTICE:
Invest a lot of time in the selection and recruitment process.

Make sure you really know what you mean by 'the best'.

Never take short cuts in hiring people.

Involve as many other people as possible in choosing the best and listen carefully to their advice.

55

Expect a lot

Your people will expect a lot of you. Expect a lot of them, too.

As a great boss you should always aim to be human. But being human doesn't necessarily mean aiming to be nice, nor aiming to please *all* the time, nor aiming to be popular.

Outside the four walls of your office is a very hostile world. Companies fall by the wayside every day. Jobs are lost. Competition will never soften, it can only but intensify.

All this might sound obvious, but it is not so to everyone. Too many people I meet in large organizations give the impression that they are cushioned from all this. They feel safe and secure within their four walls at work. They seem to think that the privilege of having a job bestows on them the precious right of having only to work 36 hours per week, of having 5 weeks' holiday each year, of having sick pay schemes. Sorry, but no such right exists. People who believe it have little sense of the harsh reality of surviving in the increasingly aggressive world of business. Ask any self-employed person. Plumbers, accountants, or consultants who fail to turn up simply do not get paid (nor do they get any more work). How could you possibly invoice someone if you haven't done the job? There can be no excuses. A self-employed person who gets stuck for two hours in a motorway traffic jam, or is suddenly afflicted with flu, or whose mother has just died cannot plead with a customer to be paid for work not done. Yet, employees of large organizations expect payment irrespective of whether they work today or not. Paying people for work not done is an expensive luxury that fewer and fewer organizations can afford. Charity, welfare, and compassion are exceptionally noble causes, but they come at an exceptionally high price. What price charity, welfare, and compassion if the end result is that you cannot deliver to your customer and have to fire your people as a result?

To survive in this vicious world, to succeed against really tough competition, you must expect a lot of your people. The reason is simple. Your *customers* will be expecting more and more of you, and if you don't deliver they will find someone else who will.

Your high expectations should permeate every facet of your people's jobs. It should be expected that they work at least the hours they are contracted to, that they give their best during this time, and that at times they even give a little bit more. You should expect your people to extend themselves by taking on additional duties as well as additional responsibilities when you're not around (no reversion to the bad old days of demarcation). You should expect initiative.

Furthermore, you should expect exceptionally high standards of behaviour and appearance (that doesn't necessarily mean suits and ties). You should expect common decency, courtesy, and good manners at all times to all people.

You should expect them to put the customer first and, furthermore, be *obsessed* with putting the customer first. In fact, you should expect them to take pure delight in putting themselves out for their customers and pleasing them.

You should expect them to be careful with the organization's money. It virtually goes without saying that you should expect them to be totally honest and trustworthy.

You should expect them to challenge you as their boss, to put you straight when you are wrong, to guide when necessary and to support you.

That's what you expect. Undoubtedly there's much more you should expect, too, but you must also look at what your people expect of *you*. It must be reciprocal. You will expect a lot of them, but they will expect a lot of you. They will expect you to behave and act in a way that is consistent with most of the 79 80 things mentioned in this book.

Occasionally, your people will *not* live up to expectations. And, from time to time, you won't either. Don't worry! It is a harsh fact of life that we do not succeed all the time. For every success there is always one failure. Even a champion athlete does not win every race, and first-rate football teams occasionally lose.

So, when you expect a lot and get a little less, don't complain. Seize the opportunity to learn – you should always expect that. Paradoxically, progress is normally made when people don't meet expectations, as their failures drive them on to even greater heights. They key is to accept the failure and progress from there, rather than delude yourself that you have succeeded, or would have succeeded if only someone else had acted in the way you expected!

First and foremost, therefore, before you expect a lot of your people, before they expect a lot from you, you must expect a lot of yourself. As soon as you start driving yourself forward in this way you will find your people driving forward with you.

PRINCIPLE:
Survival and success come from high expectations.

PRACTICE:
Spell out clearly what you expect. First, what you expect of yourself (a lot). Second, what you expect of your people (a lot). Third, find out what they expect of you (a lot). Then, strive to live up to expectations.

56

Move quickly to move ahead

You have to run fast to be one step ahead.

The world is moving faster than ever before. For some, this is frightening. What used to take weeks now takes seconds. We have the fax, the cable, the chip. The word processor I typed this book on was out of date within two months of my purchasing it. I had a boss once who would fly direct from London to Sydney for a single meeting, then fly back.

Customers won't wait. They will go to the shortest queue, and if you don't provide it, someone else will. They expect instant answers. You'll find they've taken their business elsewhere if you take ages to reply. Instant information – you'd better have access to it because you need to move rapidly to keep the business.

Increasingly, your people will expect you to move quickly, too. They will no longer be prepared to wait weeks for decisions while they see golden opportunities flying away over the horizon, to be lost forever. They will want decisions today – this is the only way you will be able to compete with the fleet-footed competition.

You have to move fast in every sense. For example, to get the best people, to retain them, and to provide the best service to your customers.

The prospect of speed can be frightening, but it can also be exhilarating. Many have yet to catch on to this. These are the people who procrastinate, who work in committees, who defer to their bosses, who take comfort in traditional hierarchies. You can be ahead of them while they're still thinking about the problem – or, even worse, talking about it.

It's all about seizing opportunities. They come thick and fast now – the new idea, someone else's initiative, a new prospect. People are impressed with speed. They like it when you call back within five minutes, write back within a day, go to see them within a week. They like it when the urgent order is delivered almost as soon as they have put the phone down. They like it when their problem is fixed the same day.

Speed is an attitude of mind. It means constantly reassessing priorities in order to put people first. It means taking pride in getting to them before others do. It means being first with the important information. It means setting up a sales presentation for tomorrow in response to today's enquiry. It means overnight stays and the occasional weekend of working. It means meeting a prospective customer on Friday and having the proposal on their desk first thing Monday.

It also means harnessing the latest in modern technology, taking advantage of even more powerful microprocessors, networking systems and communication techniques.

Speed sells. It makes people feel important. Speed is a reflection of value.

Now for the note of caution. Common sense applies. Go too fast and the damage will be too great. Don't go crazy by cutting corners and lowering quality in order to get there first. There is an optimum speed for everything – few achieve it, but it is dangerous to exceed it.

Discipline and fitness are of the essence for moving quickly. Never linger on the low-priority stuff. Never linger in meetings. Never linger on the paperwork. Concentrate on the 'people things' at work, spend time on understanding the problems of your customers and people, and then move quickly to fix them. Train yourself to think before you act, but not for too long. Always take one step back before taking three forward. Take a view, then move. In other words, train yourself to think fast by thinking clearly, quickly assimilating all the available facts, then forming a decision about whatever it is, coming to a decision as soon as possible.

Learn to read fast, scanning long documents to discover the essential points in a minute or two. Learn to communicate in clear, indisputable terms so that time is not wasted by others having to interpret the meaning of your words.

In acting fast, always keep your goal in sight. Why are you doing this? What does it achieve? By always getting there first, you develop a reputation for responsiveness and reliable service. Your customers will become committed to you, they will depend on your excellence. It will help their own business.

Your people will see it the same way. They will develop confidence in your ability to respond quickly to their needs, in providing answers to questions they find unfathomable.

Don't encumber yourself with petty problems or trivia. Don't get involved with the detail. Concentrate on important things – like working to help your people and your customers. That way you'll be able to move fast.

We live in a world of competition. It is like a race – the first to get the product to the customer wins. That should be your sole focus. It's to do with service, it's to do with quality, and that's to do with the attitudes of your people.

PRINCIPLE:
To compete successfully you must move fast.

PRACTICE:
Discipline yourself to concentrate on two priorities – acting now for your customers and acting now for your people.

57

Make the tea

Tea is one of life's great basics. Never underestimate its importance.

This is what I call the 'tea test'. For some people, the most important part of their daily routine is the next cup of tea. The world is analysed and put to rights over tea. Friendships are made and enemies identified during tea breaks.

Some companies now don't even have tea breaks. Progress has been such that people can drink tea any time they want, or coffee, or coca-cola or bottled water. But it's not progress. The smokers go off to a special room to socialize while the non-smokers drink tea at their desks and don't socialize.

In other companies electric kettles are banned and people are forced to use machines, either for the tea itself (it invariably tastes terrible) or for boiling water to pour on to tea bags (but the water is very rarely boiling).

All this is in the interest of hygiene, health and safety, and, supposedly, productivity. But it's not in the interest of treating people like human beings.

If I had a vote on this, and if I were you I would reinstate the tea break. I would change the roles (if not the rules) too. I would have the *boss* making the tea for everyone.

When you get to the fifteenth floor of the ivory tower, you will find that certain people are designated to bring the tea. Darjeeling tea is served in porcelain pots brought in on a tray with a plate of six chocolate digestive biscuits. Lemon is offered as an option to milk. Sugar is available in lumps. If it's not the secretary who serves it, it will be the contract caterer. At what price tea?

And when you get to the twentieth floor, they don't even use tea bags. Silver-plated strainers are preferred.

There is something very important about tea. It makes the world go round. How do you deal with the tea situation in your patch will be a reflection on how you see the world. Personally, I would brew the tea for everyone. Then, I'd sit down and drink with them. This would tell them the world about you. It would show them that you are not stuck on status, that you value their time as much as yours, that you recognize that they are working exceptionally hard and need to have a break a couple of times a day. Furthermore, it provides you with an invaluable opportunity to have a chat, to find out what's going on, to chew the cud on important issues, and, generally, to get to know your people that little bit better.

Now here's the tea test! Don't make tea just because it's written down in this book. The danger with books like this, and with training courses, is that people do things because they've been told to do them that way. To pass the tea test (the most important test in people management) it is very important that you make the tea because you genuinely want to do so. You have to enjoy making tea at work. You have to do it regularly (not just the day after you have read this book). You have to believe that you're no different to your people and that you are just as capable of making the tea as them.

If you are privileged to have a secretary, never ask her (or him) to make the tea, always get it yourself. Get it for her (or him) too. Also for your visitors. They'll understand. In fact, they might be quite impressed.

THE TEA TEST, ONE PASS, ONE FAILURE

During her holidays at university my daughter, Kate, undertook temporary secretarial jobs. One day the agency assigned her to a company in Bracknell. Reception told her to go to room 390. She found the room and knocked the door. Inside the room were four men, deep in conversation. One of them stared at her. "You the temp?", he asked gruffly. "Four teas please!"

The next week she was assigned to a Canadian company in Maidenhead. Her reception this time was totally different. "Hi, you must be Kate," her new boss greeted her, "let me get you some tea."

Use tea as the focal point for involving your people informally in what's going on. If you never make the tea they will think that you consider yourself to be too important, that you see yourself as being above them. Come down to their level and be level with them.

Next time you visit another section, department, or company, observe how they go about the ritual of tea. It will give you an excellent insight into how people are treated there.

PRINCIPLE:
Never expect people to make tea for you.

PRACTICE:
Always make the tea for other people.

58

Keep count

To be accountable you must count what you do.

This book is all about managing people and deliberately shies away from the numbers side of management. In fact there are many books on the financial aspects of business and many experts to help you. What's worrying, though, is that many managers become obsessed with the numbers thing. All their decisions are based on numbers. In fact, all they see of the business is numbers.

The great bosses see their business more in terms of people than numbers, but this does not mean to say that numbers are unimportant. No manager can escape from the financial objective of the bottom line and keeping a tally of progress towards it.

In other words, progress has to be quantified and measured. You don't need a mass of data to help you do this. In fact, what you need is a few common-sense measures to help you keep count of what is going on. These measures should be in your head and there should be one or, at most, two sheets of paper to summarize weekly or monthly progress.

Personally, I get excited when I look at the important numbers. Most of the time they reassure me that I can afford to eat next month. Among other things, I run a small direct mail business. I really do get a buzz when orders come in after a mailshot. All the time I want to know whether we are going to hit that target 4 per cent response rate. Jean, who runs our office, summarizes all the figures – how much we spend on printing, postage, packaging, and so on – and presents me with a one-page summary at the end of each month, showing how much profit we've made from each mailshot. It's as simple as that.

COMMON COUNTS

- **Weekly volume of units sold (by product type)**
- **Weekly sales revenue (by product type)**
- **Monthly profit margins**
- **Unit costs (cost of producing one unit)**
- **Deviations from key standards (product quality, etc.)**
- **Measures of customer satisfaction (e.g. ratios of compliments to complaints, etc.)**
- **Response times (e.g. telephone, letters, getting the job done)**
- **Delivery reliability**
- **Absentee levels**
- **Staff turnover (percentage of people leaving)**
- **Stock turnover (percentage of stock sold) by product type, etc.**

By keeping the numbers simple and meaningful, you can create a lot of interest in the business. The converse is also true. Too many managers immerse themselves in reams of complicated and irrelevant data.

Keeping count of what is going on can prove a powerful incentive to your people. The best thing to do is to make the numbers visible. Create charts and pin them up on the noticeboard, showing the number of customer complaints, the number of enquiries, response times, machine down-time, absentee levels and sales revenue.

To ensure that the measures you use are meaningful, they must relate to the projections you have in your business plan for achieving your profit objectives.

THE NUMBERS TEST: SIX KEY MEASURES

Imagine you have a new boss called Maria and she calls you in on her first day and asks you to tell her the six key measures of progress for your area of responsibility. She wants to know how these measures relate to profitability. What are you going to tell her?

Can you report to her on Monday and say what was accomplished, in quantifiable terms (against the six key measures), in the previous week?

Unless you can do so, you are in danger of being out of control and not fully accountable for what's going on.

The key is to stick to a few important numbers and to review them regularly. Make sure they are at your fingertips at all times and are updated frequently. When there are deviations from the plan, you need to be able to account for them quickly – having your answers ready before the organization zooms in on you with accusatory enquiries.

You will need to spend most of your working week dealing with the people and customer-side of the business, but you do need to devote the occasional half-hour to looking at the numbers, to reassuring yourself that progress is being made, and to reporting back to your people (and your own boss) on the results of their efforts.

PRINCIPLE:
Progress has to be quantified to justify the expenditure.

PRACTICE;
Establish a maximum of six key measures for keeping count of what you and your people accomplish week by week.

Ensure that these measures are geared to your bottom-line objectives.

Ensure that the up-to-date figures on progress are at your fingertips.

183

59

Sell yourself

Unless you can sell yourself, no one will have you!

There has been an idiomatic extension of the definition of 'selling' over recent years. Managers now have to 'sell' their ideas to employees, or to boards of directors, or to customers. The reason is very clear. Selling is all about persuading a customer to buy a product or service. The degree to which a customer can be persuaded will depend on past experience with that product and with the supplier. It will also depend on the persuasiveness of the person attempting the sale. Furthermore, there is a dependence on the helpfulness of the documentation and information provided about the product being sold. Finally, the customer has actually got to want the product.

There are many parallels here with the process of managing people. Great bosses, when in contact with their people and their own bosses, are forever in a selling mode. You might also call it lobbying, campaigning, persuading, or convincing other people. Effectively, what they are doing is selling their ideas to other people. This includes selling their interpretation of the way they see their part of the business going – in other words, they have to sell their direction. They also have to sell their beliefs in what is important. Finally, they have to sell the value of what they're doing and of the products they produce to their people.

The trend in modern management is to break organizations up into self-contained business units that have a high degree of autonomy in achieving a set of specified results. This requires managing in a businesslike way, and acceptance of the premise that all units have customers, whether they be within the organization or actually outside it. In this sense you are always in a selling mode.

It means that, from time to time, you have to justify the existence of your own unit. Unless this can be done, the unit should not exist. Why exist if you cannot demonstrate (or sell) the value your unit adds to the organization?

By accepting the premise that everyone in receipt of a service is a customer, you have to accept that everyone *supplying* that service effectively has to sell it in some way. The harsh reality is that if, in your job, you are not supplying a service, then you shouldn't be there!

THE ART OF SELLING

- Clarify who your customers and potential customers are (these will include your people, your own boss, other departments, as well as customers buying your organization's products and services)

- Listen very carefully to their requirements

- Predict their future requirements

- Clarify the products and services the people in your unit are supplying (including advice, guidance, support, information, assistance, etc.)

- Challenge yourself on what *you* are offering, and to whom (including a sense of direction, a monitoring process, motivation, etc.)

- Reconfirm your own beliefs about the value of what you and your people are supplying

- Clarify and reconfirm your own sense of the direction in which you are leading your unit

- Be totally open and honest in the above appraisal

- Be totally open and honest with your customers and your people

- Examine your own level of enthusiasm about what you do and about the products and services you have on offer. Does it show through?

- Explore with your people the initiatives that can be taken to raise the level of awareness in the minds of your customers of what you have on offer

- Focus on those people who will gain the maximum from your selling efforts

---

So, we all have customers! We all have to sell!

Regrettably, selling has a bad name. The word brings with it connotations of the second-hand car dealer who is not trustworthy, who misleads you and sells you a shining vehicle that breaks down after a few miles. However, the experts at selling will tell you that it is all about listening. It is to do with finding out about what your customers really require, how you can best help them in acquiring something they want – or even making them aware of things they might possibly want (I never really wanted a BT Chargecard until BT made me aware of its existence, but now I couldn't do without it!)

There is one further thing you need to do before you get back into the selling mode. You need to reconfirm your sense of direction. To whom are you directing your selling efforts? What is your market? There is always a danger that you squander a lot of effort selling to the wrong people. Any selling activity, therefore, has to be highly focused. You need to devote energy to those customers who are going to bring the most rewards to your organization as well as bring a lot of benefit to themselves.

To do so, sit down with your people and bring back into focus your various selling activities, no matter how indirect they might be. If necessary, develop a fresh approach to further enhance your success.

PRINCIPLE:
Selling is all about persuading a customer of the value of what you have on offer.

PRACTICE:
Review who your customers are and what you are selling them, and how you go about it.

60
Pursue crazy ideas

'If you don't feel crazy, you're not in touch with the times! The point is vital.

These are nutty times. Nutty organizations, nutty people, capable of dealing with the fast, fleeting, fickle, are a requisite for survival.'
(Tom Peters, *Liberation Management*, Macmillan, 1992)

Just look around you. You won't have to look far to see the product of some crazy idea, whether it be your laptop computer or your portable CD player.

Look around you and identify the people you find most interesting. Often it will be those 'slightly crazy' people who wear outrageous ties, tell outrageous stories, and do outrageous things. They go beyond the boundaries of normality. But normality and craziness are just perceptions, points of view (for example, are men wearing earrings, women wearing trousers, women bathing topless normal or crazy?).

Progress is all about extending the boundaries of what we perceive to be normal. In the first half of this century, it was *not* normal to watch television. Then it became the norm to watch one channel only, then two, then three and four. Now we have a choice of over 30 channels, and that will become the norm, along with interactive television. The concept of a choice of 30 television channels would have seemed crazy to people living in the 1950s (it is still crazy to some people now!).

A great boss exploits the craziest of ideas to push back the boundaries of normality, because it is the maintenance of normality that, in the end, paradoxically, destroys. This is because the maintenance of normality gives people a false sense of security and, more frequently, bores. Conversely, the pursuit of crazy ideas excites people, motivates them. So, get out and about and kick around some crazy ideas, then kick them off and score a few goals.

You will be amazed at the buzz this creates around you. Don't be put off by those miserable cynics with a well-worn line of patter that goes something like this: 'We've seen it all before, it won't work, this will cause immense problems, no one will go along with it!' Remember how trade unions used to operate 20 years ago?

There is no future in normality. One of the things a great boss must do is go beyond the boundaries of normality (and I'm not talking of antisocial behaviour, or illegal activity, or immorality in any shape or form).

Every organization creates its own Berlin Wall, but the great boss breaks it down. The result might well be chaos in the short term, but long-term progress will be made.

CRAZY (AWAY) DAYS

- No agenda
- Choose a crazy venue (a conference room at the local zoo, say)
- Do crazy things (as the boss, you serve the food)
- Anybody interested can attend
- Nothing legal banned (say what you like)
- Select the craziest person in the team and give him or her an award
- Look at other organizations' crazy ideas (Virgin, Apple, The Body Shop, etc.)
- Generate crazy ideas for taking the business forward
- Select your craziest customer and send him or her an award
- Give a prize for the craziest idea
- Pick on at least one crazy idea to be implemented
- Everything negative banned (only work on ideas you are definitely going to take forward)

It would be crazy for this author to suggest some crazy ideas. The one I love best is to destroy 95 per cent of the paper that clogs up your operation. People who write memos are *really* crazy! Inverting pyramids is not so crazy, but it would be if you (the boss) worked in reception, made the tea or even cleaned the toilets. Is it crazy to live in the real world, to understand what it's really like to clean toilets?

Equally satisfying is to do some crazy things for your customers (send them birthday cards – is that crazy?) or for your staff (send them to Hawaii to look at a similar operation there – the benefits will be enormous).

Write a book about all the crazy things you have done. It will sell! (Read Ricardo Semler's *Maverick*, Century, 1993).

PRINCIPLE:
Living in a crazy world requires crazy people.

Progress is made by implementing crazy ideas.

To be normal is abnormal, to be abnormal should become the norm.

The reservoir of crazy ideas is inexhaustible.

PRACTICE:
At least once every six months, select and implement one or more crazy ideas generated by you and your people to help further the business.

61

Pay well

To get the best results, you must have the best people. To have the best people you must pay the best.

There is an inexorable logic about the above statement. It is the same as the cliché: 'Pay peanuts, get monkeys'. Again it is common sense at work!

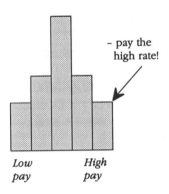

– pay the high rate!

Low pay   High pay

Market survey of pay rates

Too many employers fail to see the efficacy of this logic. All they see are costs that have to be reduced to maximize profits. People are costs, so their ugly logic is to keep pay levels to a bare minimum.

Here's another common-sense cliché: 'In our business, people are our greatest asset'. You *have* to invest in people to reap long-term dividends. Assets have to be maintained and developed to sustain and increase their value.

At work, people need to feel valued. No matter what fine words you use as an expression of appreciation, no matter what fine training you give them, ultimately people will gauge their value by what you pay them. That value will be relative. Your people will make comparisons with the market and where appropriate, will trade intrinsic job satisfaction for real money. No matter how noble people are in sacrificing pay in favour of vocational ambition, they still have to pay the mortgage. Charity, loyalty, and an employee's goodwill should never be exploited at the expense of pay.

The key is to ensure that people do not divert their precious energies into squabbling over pay. Ideally, you want people to forget about pay so that they concentrate their efforts on producing excellent results. The best bosses keep a step ahead by awarding pay increases before they're asked for. They take the initiative in surveying the market, in ensuring that the pay of their people (whatever their grade) is up there with the best.

It's obvious that as soon as people start feeling bad about pay, there will be a risk that the best will leave for more money. However take care. You can pay well and *still* get it wrong! A system of individual performance-related pay is one way of doing so! Dangling carrots in front of people is *not* good remuneration practice. You should assume that people are going to give of their best and will not be able to give more, even if you pay them more. There is much evidence to suggest that the 'carrot and stick' theory of motivation does not work, so why attempt to use it?

The amount you pay must be relative to the market. We work and live in a hostile, aggressive world where competition is the name of the game. The real competition is for scarce, valuable resources to deliver first-class results. The real competition is to have the best people on board with you and to reward them with a fair share of the financial success to which they contribute. So, if you want to link pay to performance, then link everyone's pay to the success of that part of the business for which they are jointly responsible. Use your business plan as a vehicle for this.

In paying well, don't mess around with complicated allowances, individual bonus schemes, or payments in kind. Keep it simple – just pay a high salary or wage! The more complicated you make it, the more argument and dissent you will cause.

The ideal practice is to have your people share in the ownership of the business. In that way they reap a fair and equitable dividend geared directly to their own efforts.

Never be swayed by the accountants that you *can't* afford to pay well. The converse argument is true: you can't afford *not* to pay well.

PRINCIPLE:
Pay is a reflection of how you value people.

Individual performance-related pay is divisive and unfair.

PRACTICE:
Survey the market and ensure that your people are paid in the upper quartile of the going rate.

Link everyone's pay to the performance of the business unit in which they work.

Always take the initiative on pay. Never wait for your people to demand increases.

62

Don't let the side down

When bosses let their people down, their loyalty and mutual trust is eroded.

I have heard senior executives stand up in front of audiences and criticize the very people who immediately report to them. I have also come across managers who promise they will do something for their people and don't.

Loyalty is a precious commodity. It can easily be lost when you let your people down. People should never be loyal to the organizations they work for. After all, organizations are impersonal entities that hire and fire people depending on circumstances. Loyalty only applies to the relationships between people. Great bosses are very loyal to their people and, conversely, their people are incredibly loyal to them.

Establishing loyalty requires an incredibly high standard of personal management. It means that you have to give without any consideration of taking. It means that you always back your people in their pursuit of their work goals. First and foremost, it means that you never let them down.

When you speak in public, you will have nothing but praise for your people. If you feel otherwise, then a public platform is *not* the place to raise your concerns. Openness and honesty are fine, but even these two important principles have a place, and, in the first place, you should deal directly with the people who concern you. Never let them down by dealing indirectly with the problem by airing it in public.

Your people will be very sensitive about the extent to which you support them. They will expect you to fight their corner with your own boss and will feel let down if you fail to deliver what they believe is necessary. They will expect you to behave in a way that is consistent with the elevated standards they demand of you as a boss. For example, they will expect you to watch your language and not swear too often. If you demean yourself they will feel let down. As the boss they will put you on a pedestal. You will fail them if you step down off it and indulge in uproarious dirty jokes.

Another example is if you give interviews on television, radio, or to the newspaper. Your people will take pride in your performance and will feel let down if you don't come across too well.

The same with important visitors to the factory or the office. Your people will expect you to behave in a certain way, to take the lead in giving visitors a warm welcome, in introducing everyone to them. They will feel let down if you neglect to give these visitors due attention.

The reality is that your people want you to succeed. You are their figurehead and, in their eyes, you are carrying out onerous duties that they find a little foreboding. They will feel let down if you fail in these important duties.

What you have to do as a boss is to live up to these expectations of your people. Anything else and they will be disappointed. Job descriptions rarely reflect such expectations and, in most cases, are quite useless. Clarifying expectations and ensuring that yours converge with theirs is, therefore, a vital role for you as a boss.

Whatever the textbooks say, whatever your organization decrees, in this day and age you cannot impose your own definition of how you should act as a boss on your people. It has to evolve gradually, with them, in order that a high degree of mutual understanding can be achieved.

You might think that allowing your people to put you on a pedestal will make you distant from them. In fact, you need to get very close to them to understand what that pedestal is all about. You need to develop an in-depth appreciation of your respective expectations with them, of how each one of you is to go about your task. With this understanding, the probability that you will let the side down will be minimized and, even if you make mistakes and fail occasionally, they will not see it as letting them down but just as making mistakes, which all human beings do from time to time.

The closer you get to your people, the more you all get to understand and accept your various expectations of each other and the greater the loyalty there will be between you.

PRINCIPLE:
Mutual loyalty and mutual understanding.

PRACTICE:
Get close to your people to develop an understanding of what will cause them to feel let down.

63

Provide energy

Keep on recharging your team's batteries!

The worst bosses drain their people of all energy. They run them into the ground, suck them dry, and take advantage of their goodwill. It is exploitative management.

People need to be energized. Few of us are that self-sufficient that we can consistently draw on our own valuable resources to drive us forward day in and day out.

Great bosses are past masters at injecting energy into groups of people, reinvigorating them.

The central source of energy is a positive attitude towards your people. They sense it, respect it. This is reinforced through other sources, which a great boss secures to revitalize people. For example, a boss who goes out of the way to obtain vital new equipment for his (or her) people will energize them. So will a boss who strives to invent new and meaningful ways of rewarding the group's achievements, or who inspires them with his (or her) creativity, incisive thinking, and real support. Training can also be a vital source, enabling people to get away and be energized by some novel learning experience of direct relevance to their work. Humour and fun in the everyday situation can be ingredients, too. The great bosses have an innate ability to utter one funny word that can spark a flagging group of people back to life!

SOURCES OF ENERGY

- A positive attitude towards your people
- Physical resources (all types: money, people, equipment)
- Reward
- Inspiration
- Training
- Humour
- Competition (light-hearted)
- Competition (surviving on the edge)
- Competition (simply winning)
- Food (team lunches)
- Celebration
- Fear
- Change (stimulus)
- Travel
- Challenge (extending yourself)
- Recognition
- Demonstrable pride
- Gossip/grapevine
- Trust (sharing confidences)
- Giving space (allowing people their heads)

Competition is also a source of energy. A good boss will frequently remind people of the competition and the need to beat it to survive. There is nothing that energizes people more than the prospect of being outclassed by competitors.

Just getting your people together for an informal lunch can have an energizing effect, as does celebrating achievement. Fear is another factor. In this day and age, no boss will attempt to create fear unnecessarily, but the reality is that we all have to fear the consequences of losing our jobs through mediocrity and lacklustre performance. A good boss will bring that into focus, too.

Other opportunities can be to provide a source of 'stimulus', enabling people to move away from the routines, to travel, to enjoy new work experiences, and to meet people from elsewhere, even customers! All these things can be tremendously invigorating.

THE TONIC

'I've had bosses in the past whom I would avoid like the plague. Our new boss is different. Strange as it seems, I look forward to every encounter with him. I always walk away after a session with him feeling really good, feeling I'm really going to give everything now to please him. He always seems to understand, he's always encouraging. Furthermore, he's always got interesting new things to say. I am learning a lot from him. I find his own enthusiasm infectious. When you feel down, you don't have to tell him, he senses it, he reassures you. He's a tonic!'

Pride and recognition also come into the energy equation, as does a boss who will take you into his (or her) confidence, who will actually trust you as well as feed you with those fascinating titbits of gossip before others do.

Finally, the most energizing thing a boss can do is set you a huge challenge and give you the space in which to achieve it!

PRINCIPLE:
People need to be energized to succeed.

PRACTICE:
Continually recreate opportunities to develop a 'feel good' climate among your people.

Reinforce their will to succeed.

Reinforce your own will to succeed.

64

Say 'Thank you'

There is a far greater need for appreciation than most people appreciate.

Appreciation is a rare commodity. When was the last time your own boss expressed genuine appreciation for all your efforts? When was the last time you expressed genuine appreciation for all your people's efforts?

Expressing appreciation is a precious skill. If you go around saying 'Thank you' every two minutes, then the currency gets devalued, people won't believe you, they will think you're trying to get something out of them. Conversely, if you never say 'Thank you', your people will become downhearted, will feel that all their efforts are to no avail, are not recognized, are not valued. All too often, people complain that the only time they see their bosses is when things go wrong and they receive a telling off.

The large majority of people work exceptionally hard, handling difficult situations, dealing with demanding customers, fixing intractable problems, but their labours often go unnoticed by bosses, who spend hours in the ivory tower involved in meetings that never take them anywhere. Few of us like going around waving flags in front of our bosses saying 'Didn't we do well?' – we are too proud for that. Some people are glory seekers, but their glory is devalued by the mere act of demanding it. Recognition, glory, appreciation – all are worth more if they are unsolicited, if they come unexpectedly.

What you must do as a great boss is go and seek out and express appreciation for the great things your people are doing. Great can be small. It might be the great way someone at the front line handles

A THOUSAND WAYS OF SAYING 'THANK YOU'

The first 20 examples.

- Send a 'Thank you' card
- Write a 'Thank you' memo
- Pin a 'Thank you' notice on the noticeboard
- Add a 'Thank you' note to your Christmas cards
- Send birthday cards to each of your people and add a 'Thank you'
- Take the team out for lunch and make a 30-second 'Thank you' speech
- Give a pat on the back (or, more precisely, on the shoulder)
- Go out of your way to see someone, shake hands, and say 'Thank you for all your efforts' in a measured way
- Send a 'Thank you' letter to their home (the family will be impressed)
- Bring in some cakes as a gesture of appreciation
- Make a gift (bottle of whisky, perfume, etc.) as a vote of thanks
- Send flowers
- Produce formal certificates of 'Thanks' and have them framed
- Give everyone a watch inscribed with appropriate 'Thank you' words
- Throw a dinner to which partners are invited and make a speech mentioning every individual and thanking them for their contributions
- Mention people in dispatches, say, writing to your own boss referring to the excellent efforts of your people, and copy the letter to your people
- Ring someone up and say 'Thank you'
- Say 'Thank you' to an individual in front of the Chief Executive or other important people
- Make an effort to wander around and say 'Thank you'
- etc.

an abusive customer. It might be the initiative your receptionist took in helping a customer whose car had broken down outside. It might be the extra hours your people put in to complete an urgent mailshot. It might be the way your people rallied together to cover the job of a colleague who went sick. It might be the excellent display your people put on for the Chairman's walk around. It might be when someone stood in for you at the last minute on a speaking engagement and performed exceptionally well. It might be consistently achieving your weekly targets over the last three months.

I could go on, but there must be a thousand opportunities to express appreciation. Remember, your people are not machines. Day in and day out they will be working in an exceptional way, sorting out unexpected problems to keep the operation going. It is critical that you recognize this, appreciate it, and, furthermore, value it.

This is the simple message put across in Kenneth Blanchard and Spencer Johnson's excellent book *The One Minute Manager* (Collins Willow, 1983): 'People who feel good about themselves produce good results', and, elsewhere, 'Help people reach their full potential, catch them doing something right'.

Managing people is an art. You therefore have to use all your creative energies to find the most appropriate ways in which to say 'Thank you'. What is right for one group of people might be wrong for another. Saying 'Thank you' doesn't require vast expenditure; all it requires is genuine, heartfelt appreciation for others' efforts and a genuine desire to express this.

PRINCIPLE:
Recognition and expression of appreciation.

PRACTICE:
Seek the good things that your people are doing and find some inventive way of saying 'Thank you'.

Avoid saying 'Thank you' as of a routine; always vary the approach.

65

Get your facts right

Facts are elusive creatures – they come disguised in many forms.

You have to walk a thin line between naïveté and suspicion. When you have created a climate of openness, honesty, and trust, the easiest thing in the world is to take stated facts at face value. Conversely, when you are unsure about a person, it is natural to doubt their word, to probe for misrepresentation, and to try to establish whether or not there's an ulterior motive.

The truth is an elusive commodity. It is rarely a set of simple facts presented on one sheet of paper. It comes dressed up in different guises or takes on different shapes. Sometimes it is hidden beneath distortions and exaggerations.

The truth is that facts are rarely as they seem. They have to be viewed in different lights, and the danger is seeing them in one light only. It is also well known that our senses are overwhelmed with a mass of data every day and that we only allow to filter through that which we want, rejecting the rest.

Given all this, it is hardly surprising that frequently we do not get our facts right, that we misunderstand, or base our judgements on incomplete information, or take as gospel what someone has told us, or reject some important piece of news because it has been conveyed by someone we don't trust or don't like.

Handling information passed to and from us is one of the most critical skills for a great boss. To get anything done successfully, it is imperative that we get our facts right. Without sounding too moralistic or religious, the probability is that if we deliberately set out to mislead, distort, or manipulate, then we will eventually get found out. The same applies even when we are innocent but inadvertently mislead, distort, or manipulate. Our credibility will suffer accordingly.

There are a minority of people we come across who can *never* see the facts, or the truth, for what it is. These are the irrational people who wear red spectacles and see red whatever you present to them. They are incredibly difficult people to deal with because they never accept what you or other people say – no matter how glaringly obvious and factual it is – but, rather, always cling to their own coloured, limited, and, frequently, distorted version of the facts. Turn on your television and just study one or two of our politicians for elaboration on this point.

Furthermore, in handling facts, it is easy to assume that we have them all to hand. Part of the skill is to recognize that we rarely have a complete picture and have to make judgements based on incomplete information. Too many people jump to the conclusion that because it was fact in the past, it will be fact in the future. Business is all about risk and, despite our considerable learning from experience, there is no guarantee that a certain sequence of events, or pattern of behaviours that occurred in the past will, under the same conditions, recur in the future. There are no future facts.

Part of the skill in handling facts is to differentiate *fact* from *opinion*. Too many people confuse the two, so that, for example, they take it as a fact that 'Richard is lazy' or that 'Norma is incompetent'. This extends to how facts are interpreted. The fact that 'Richard rarely volunteers to help' does not necessarily mean that he is, for a fact, lazy. The key is to get at 'core' facts, which can withstand scrutiny and challenge.

By getting at the core facts, we are in a much better position to make effective decisions. Core facts are tangible entities, things that have actually happened. They are immutable. These tangible entities can either be described using accurate language or measured in some quantitative way. It is a fact that Julie has been late on three occasions in the last fortnight. It is not a fact that she is *always* unpunctual. It is a fact that the new truck broke down on the motorway on its very first journey. It is not a fact that the new truck is useless and the company should have gone for another make. It is a fact that Norma frequently forgets things. It is not a fact that she is incompetent.

FACT-FINDING SKILLS

- **Eliminating subjectivity (not personalizing the information you receive)**
- **Differentiating interpretation from fact**
- **Separating opinion from fact**
- **Resisting value judgements (not jumping to personal conclusions)**
- **Seeking out facts (identifying reliable sources)**
- **Double-checking the information**
- **Understanding the meaning and relevance of the information**
- **Completing the picture (obtaining all available information)**
- **Questioning and testing (the source of information)**
- **Cleaning out the sieve (opening the mind)**
- **Being prepared to handle unpalatable and unpleasant information (which hurts us)**
- **Knowingly taking risks when not all the facts are available**

Getting the facts right is about relationships and trust. It is about making judgements about who can prove a reliable source of information and who is untrustworthy. We learn from bitter experience.

It is also about not allowing our personal beliefs and views to cloud or distort the information we receive. Some facts *will* hurt us. These are the unpalatable truths of life that we hide from, which are in danger of destroying our self-confidence and lowering the elevated image we have of ourselves. In other words, we have a natural tendency to protect ourselves from information that will damage us. It is a dangerous tendency because, by facing up to the unpleasant facts of life, we become more able to deal with them and less prone to being damaged by them.

The key, therefore, is to ensure that any information we receive is not taken personally. If we do so, then the 'messenger' will feel under attack (because of our defensiveness) and is less likely to provide us with helpful information in the future.

So, rise above any attempt at personal or subjective interpretation of the facts whenever you receive them.

PRINCIPLE:
Facts are the basis for effective decisions.

PRACTICE:
Develop your skills in getting at the core facts irrespective of their personal impact on you.

66

Argue well

Argue with your boss, argue with your people, argue with your colleagues, but do it constructively.

There is a great virtue in arguing, and major disadvantages in not doing so.

Argument, if conducted in a positive, healthy, and non-personal manner is effective in dragging out the truth, in converging on common-sense solutions and exposing people for what they really are.

Argument is the embodiment of verbal challenge. Not all of us are that perfect that we are above challenge. Argument will improve us and will improve others too. It helps us learn more about ourselves as well as about the people we work with. It helps us examine our own beliefs and values, our own opinions and prejudices.

Avoidance of argument leads to dogma. People become fixed in their views, believe they are always right. It results in rhetoric and alienation. People avoid raising certain issues for fear of an emotional backlash. People who don't argue close their minds to the potential of a greater wisdom.

Avoidance of argument is prevalent in traditional hierarchical organizations where deference to status is preferred to open debate.

The best bosses are prepared to argue their corner with anyone, irrespective of status. They are prepared to accept the challenge and, furthermore, happy to challenge others. The key is never to make it personal, never to get at people for holding opposing views, or undeveloped views.

As soon as you stop arguing with the people around you, you will begin to lose touch with reality. You will begin to close your mind and interpret life in your own sweet way. You will fail to understand why people behave in a manner that is totally contradictory to your own beliefs and values. You will close in on yourself and produce your own dogma.

While argument should always be welcomed care should be taken in the way it is conducted. As mentioned above, the points you make should never be personal. In other words, you should take care to avoid injecting too much negative emotion into the argument. *Positive* emotions, such as passion and enthusiasm, are fine, and sometimes sufficiently infectious to sway your colleagues in favour of your case, but negative emotions, such as anger and irritation, will only serve to dampen the argument and alienate. Argument is best conducted at an intellectual level. It is all about the exploration and resolution of apparently opposing views in order to converge on a way forward that everyone, collectively, can subscribe to.

The great bosses, therefore, welcome argument – in fact, they love it. Their people will welcome it, too, because the end result is that they will know exactly where they stand.

The challenge to you as a boss is to generate the arguments for and against certain key issues that require an imminent decision. Get among your people and let them argue it out whether they should have new uniforms, wear name badges, use precious money from the budget to redecorate the office. Let them argue it out whether the company should invest in a new copying machine. Present your own ideas to them and let them argue with you, telling you it is unwise to change the shift rota, to initiate yet another training programme on customer service, or whatever.

Arguing with your people does not necessarily mean letting them reach their own conclusions. Sometimes, quite rightly, you will have made up your mind on the best course of action. You will then need to argue your case with your people. The only option they have is to persuade you that there is a better course of action to closing down 'A' plant and saving a million pounds per year.

The process of argument will force you to get your facts right, to make sure that you know what you're talking about. It will also make you completely aware of what your people are thinking and enable you to be sensitive to it. It will also force you to justify, in clear, unequivocal terms, the basis of your decisions.

One of the valuable results of arguing is that it does end up with certain people changing their minds. Don't be frightened of doing so yourself. As a boss, you are a human being and you are quite entitled to alter your view if you are persuaded by a better argument. However, if you do so too often, people will come to the conclusion that you have no mind of your own. As with most things in life, there is a delicate balance to be reached.

Enjoy the argument, too. Always laugh and smile when you disagree with someone or they disagree with you. If there is any danger of the argument becoming heated, crack a joke, a smile. This can readily diffuse the situation and indicate that there is nothing personal in what's being said.

Don't be frightened of disagreement – encourage it. The best route to agreement is through disagreement and argument!

PRINCIPLE:
Argument is a valuable tool for deciding on the best of a number of options.

PRACTICE:
Whenever a decision is required on a difficult issue, get among your people and encourage them to argue it out.

67

Cut out paper

Paper is the tool of the lazy manager, the coward, and the bureaucrat.

Paper does have some really good uses. You are staring at one right now. Now, proceed to your in-tray and challenge yourself to identify some really bad uses. That's the easy bit. Pass over to your out-tray and critically examine its contents. Eliminate at least half of it. That's the difficult bit.

Never use paper when word of mouth will do. Get on the phone, go and see the person. Don't write memos. Don't complain on paper.

Use paper to good effect, which means finding its positive uses – like expressing appreciation, summarizing complex arguments, and supporting them with concise data.

Use paper to help you think things through – the process of writing something down can help you clarify your thoughts – but don't use paper to impose your thinking on others. Instead, use it to present options, arguments, and recommendations. Use paper to present information for others to study.

Don't write stupid memos. Don't allow yourself to be trapped into recording trivia. Don't use paper as 'I told you so' insurance policies just in case something goes wrong and someone didn't take your advice.

Here's something I'm going to preach but I don't practise too well myself. Have a regular purge on files. Clear them out. You know which files you regularly refer to. Get rid of the rest.

Don't pretend it will get any better with electronic mail and data storage. The same arguments apply. In fact, substituting computer screens for paper merely accentuates the problem and requires more discipline in eliminating verbiage and unnecessary recorded information.

Think carefully about whom you circulate copies to. There is a tendency everywhere to moan about ineffective communication and to react by swamping people with more boring paper. There are better ways to communicate than by circulating paper. Often people are too busy and don't read properly what's on the paper. There is a limit to the amount of written information the human brain can absorb in any one period of time.

You can always judge a person's effectiveness by the amount of paper and clutter in their office. Enter the office of a really great boss and you will see relatively little paper on the desk. The point is that you cannot manage by accumulating paper. Issuing instructions on paper is a demonstration of distrust. Producing big thick policy manuals is the same.

Paper is often used because bosses don't credit their people with common sense. If you rely on people's common sense, you won't need to write them silly instructions.

Treat paper as a priceless commodity. Use it rarely. Assess carefully whatever you put on to paper. Use it for positive purposes only. Try to make each document a work of art. Keep the number of pages down to a bare minimum. Even so, summarize what you're going to say, then say it. Use appendices so that the boring stuff can be put at the back and doesn't interrupt the flow.

PAPERWORK TO BAN

- **Memos**
- **Written instructions**
- **Records of opinion**
- **Self-justifications**
- **'Insurance' documents ('I told you so, I'm therefore covering my backside')**
- **Complaints about anyone**
- **Policy manuals**

POSITIVE PAPERWORK

- Letters of appreciation (compliments, praise, etc.)
- Summary data
- Your own personal notes
- Presentations of different options for moving forward
- Agendas
- Summary records of formal meetings
- Plans (business plans, strategies, etc.)
- Formal notices (statutory regulations, etc.)
- Invitations (to attend training sessions, etc.)
- Training material
- Formal contracts

The key is personal discipline. Avoid taking the easy way out by rushing into print. Try to resist putting things on to paper just because someone else has. Always respond, but not always in writing. Pick up the telephone or wander down two floors to see the person who sent you a memo.

If the issue is difficult and complicated, you must go and see whoever is involved and talk it through with them, rather than have an endless exchange of memos. Resist venting your anger, having goes at people, on paper.

Put simply, use paper positively.

PRINCIPLE:
Use paper with due care and consideration.

PRACTICE:
Only use paper as a last resort. As a first resort pick up the telephone or go to see the person involved.

68

Go away!

The only real way to prove that your people are as good as you think they are is to go away for a while and let them get on with it!

I know from my own experience that when my boss went away I breathed a sigh of relief. It was a sense of freedom, a feeling that I could now get on and do my real job without fear of interruption. Somehow, my bosses always made me feel guilty – though not intentionally – if I stepped out of line and did something different. For example, I would work long hours most days, but occasionally I would leave early. That would be the very day my boss, who had been unavailable all day, would leave me a note saying, 'I dropped by to see you at 4.55 p.m.'. This was five minutes after I had left.

Furthermore, when my boss was around I felt I had to do things that would please him (I never had a woman as a boss). When he was away, I could please myself in the way I went about my job. I could experiment, I could even make decisions without having to account to him step by step. I could even do his job for him. In fact, my first trip to America was on that basis. My boss was on holiday for three weeks. During that time, the company I worked for took over a small company in San Francisco. It had been a well-kept secret until that point. If my boss had been present, he would have considered the takeover sufficiently important for him to go to California to deal with the personnel side, but he wasn't around, so I decided to go instead. I just told people I was going and then fixed it. No one stopped me. I left a note for my boss for his return and, when I came back, I gave him a full report. He didn't object and I don't think I screwed up.

So, just go away! It presents your people with immense opportunities to develop their own skills, to be accountable for their own decisions.

WHERE TO GO

- **On a three-week holiday (obviously)**
- **On a three-week senior management development programme at a business school**
- **On a sabbatical (of six months)**
- **On a major project, researching something of strategic importance to the organization**
- **Tell your own boss to take three weeks off and go and do his or her job**
- **Go and run the company's operations in the Dutch Antilles for three months**
- **Travel the country (world), auditing the organization's operations**
- **Get yourself assigned to another department as an internal consultant**
- **Get seconded to another department**
- **Participate in a job swap with another organization**
- **Sit at home and write a book about the organization (or some aspect of it)**
- **Spend four weeks arranging some major conference for the organization**

When you return you will be amazed at how your people have blossomed, at what they have achieved in your absence.

Inevitably, you will feel vulnerable, saying to yourself, 'Am I really needed around here; what is my true role?'

The answer is that going away is the biggest test of your success as a boss. If you have developed your people in the way you believe you should have done, if you have given them the responsibilities they are capable of discharging, if you have allowed them their head as you know you should, then all that will have been adequately tested during your absence.

It has to happen some time. If you go sick, or take leave to have a baby the issue will be forced.

You can decide who should deputize for you (if at all). Some bosses rotate the deputyship, to ensure a fair share of elevated responsibility.

Your role as a boss is to create a group of people round you who are self-sufficient, who can place little reliance on you for decision making. Your role is to provide a framework within which they can work. But, remember, you yourself are not the framework. So, by going away you don't actually remove that framework. As a boss you provide direction, but direction should not change within three weeks or three months. Even if there is a crisis, your people will be as good as you at handling it, and if it's a *major* crisis, they will call you back. Many crises, in any event, are predictable and you wouldn't be going away anyway if you thought one was about to happen.

Going away is a test of confidence, a test of confidence in yourself as well as in your people. It is a test of having done well, of saying to yourself, 'I've established a great group of people round me, which really is an achievement, but now I want them to confirm how great they are'.

They will miss you. When you return, you can focus on what they have achieved in your absence. So, your return becomes a trigger for celebration!

PRINCIPLE:
Your absence enables people to really prove themselves.

PRACTICE:
Create an opportunity to disappear from your office (for at least three weeks) on a regular basis.

69

Demonstrate your beliefs

People need to know what you're made of.

One of the central common-sense themes in this book is that you have to be yourself as a boss. Too many managers allow their *organizations* to define what they're all about, what they should stand for, what they should believe in.

Nobody should be able to tell you what to think. As a boss (along with your people) you should be able to think for yourself. Regrettably, too much modern management practice is based on the assumption that *we* (in senior positions) have to tell *them* (lower down in the organization) what to think, how to behave, and what sort of attitudes to adopt. In fact, there is a vast consultancy industry that helps organizations change cultures and attitudes. It is almost as if some 'God-like' figure up there in the top reaches of the organization has defined the perfect attitude, the perfect culture, and is now undertaking a 'change process' to make everyone conform with the prescribed perfection.

As mentioned in other sections of this book, modern managers should be preoccupied with defining 'what' people have to achieve and allowing them a high degree of discretion in deciding 'how' best to achieve 'what' they have to. Furthermore, modern managers should provide support to help their people achieve their goals. However, that is a 'belief' that I, the author, have. My belief is that managers should provide a supportive role to their people to achieve well-defined objectives, for their organization. What is your belief?

Throughout our lives we develop a belief and value system that helps guide us along the tortuous paths we choose (or are forced) to tread. Problems arise when these beliefs and values conflict with those of others. To use an extreme example, the beliefs and values of a thief or a mugger will inevitably conflict with our own.

However, beliefs and values frequently cannot be packaged into clear-cut 'rights' and 'wrongs'. There is a wide spectrum of beliefs and values across which there is a subtle range of variations. You might believe it is important to 'care for your people'. However, what *you* believe constitutes 'care' might well vary substantially from your *boss's* belief. You might believe that caring for people means keeping absentees who are long-term sick permanently on the payroll. Your boss might be thinking the opposite, believing that the considerable expense of paying the long-term sick puts the whole operation at risk, so the most caring solution is to keep the majority in jobs and sack the long-term sick.

Another example could be that you believe that the most important thing you can do is devote a substantial part of your time to your customers. Your people might believe you don't spend enough time with them. These beliefs and values conflict.

Beliefs and values reflect what you consider to be important in the conduct of your everyday work. Regrettably, many bosses are not aware of their beliefs and values and would be unable to articulate them clearly.

We are surreptitiously conditioned by the people round us – by our parents, bosses and our peers, our own organizations, and society at large – to hold certain values and believe in certain things. The world is flat and performance appraisal is good for you are two examples. These beliefs enter our bloodstream, often without us realizing, and form the basis of our own behaviours at work and home. In the 1990s many people believe it is acceptable for a man and woman who are not married to live together, to even have children outside of wedlock. Fifty years ago, most people believed that such a practice was unacceptable.

In a world where beliefs and values are rapidly changing and there is increasing confusion about them, it is critical that each one of us establish our own set, and develop and apply them.

As a boss, you will be under constant observation. Your people will be informally monitoring everything you do to establish what you are really made of, whether you are your own person or whether you are a puppet of the organization, merely echoing what the organization thinks.

In my view, it is critical to establish clearly what you believe is important in the way you go about your work, and to demonstrate this consistently to your people – not just through your words, but also through your actions.

The greatest leaders are those who have a strong set of beliefs, not only in what they have to achieve, but also in how to achieve it. These beliefs often bring them into conflict with authority – and that's when, occasionally, you have to put your job on the line (see Section 52). While we are taught to respect authority, there does come a time in life when it has to be questioned. This is when you have to pit your strongly held set of beliefs against those represented by that authority.

However, such a demonstration of beliefs is not aimed at conflict but at convergence. You will find that you work best as a boss when your own beliefs and values are shared by the people you work with. Demonstrating your beliefs should not be a process of writing them down and getting your people to agree. Far better for it to be an evolutionary process whereby you learn about each other's beliefs and values through your words and actions and gradually converge on a set that is not only shared but consistently put into practice.

PRINCIPLE:
Your beliefs reflect what is important to you.

PRACTICE:
Ensure that every word you utter, every single thing you do, is consistent with your own beliefs on how you should go about your work.

Listen carefully to others and, through debate, allow your beliefs to evolve (if they become fixed they become dogma).

Never allow other people (or your organization) to impose their beliefs on you.

Never attempt to impose your beliefs on others.

70

Always ask your people

Your people are less likely to question your decisions if you ask their opinion beforehand.

Your decision? No, it will be *our* decision! The probability is that you will come to the wrong decision unless you ask your people about it first. While you might, ultimately, be accountable for the decision and its implementation, there is no reason for not sharing the process of making that decision.

Too many managers have this macho idea that they have to make snap decisions to be effective. They rush in, make up their minds very quickly, then declare their decision to their people, who shake their heads in disbelief. It takes brave people to stand up to bosses who think they know best and persuade them to change their mind.

Always ask your people first. This doesn't mean an endless number of meetings, or working parties, or steering groups – just a little common sense. If the decision affects them, ask them! Don't convene a meeting, just go to see them and find out what they think.

As a boss, you can only have a relatively limited perspective of what's going on, at best an overview. You will not be able to see *all* the pros and cons. More often than not, your people will know best. They are closer to the operation than you are, will know the problems, will know the solutions.

Never delude yourself that you know best. You don't. Your job is to get a sensible decision made, not necessarily make it yourself. Your

---

ASKING FOR AGGRAVATION

'The problem with our boss (the Production Manager) is that he is always having to reverse his decisions. Last week, for example, the Operations Director called him in and said there had been a request from Sales to manufacture an urgent order for one of our major customers – Smith and Brown Ltd. They need five tons of our Special Grade 'A' material by the end of the week.

Our boss told the Director that it would be done. He came back and told us to amend our schedules and do it. We pointed out the consequences. It would mean a major changeover and the loss of three hours' production and letting other customers down.

He accused us of being difficult, of being negative, of not putting the customer first, of creating problems. There was a stand-off while he said he'd think about it. Meanwhile, one of our production supervisors rang up his mate at Smith and Brown. He knows them quite well because he's been up there to sort out some of their technical problems. Our supervisor found out that Smith and Brown's deadline was actually four days later than they had given us. They had built in some buffer to be on the safe side – knowing that we're not 100 per cent reliable on deliveries.

We had a changeover scheduled for the weekend and were planning to run the Special Grade 'A' on the Monday. There would be no problem in running an extra five tons. It could be shipped overnight and Smith and Brown Ltd would have it first thing Tuesday morning – well within their required time scales.

Eventually our boss went back to Sales, who talked to Smith and Brown. They confirmed Tuesday would be all right as they weren't going to use the material before Thursday.

If only he'd asked us in the first place, a lot of aggro could have been prevented.'

---

job is to endorse your people's decisions and be accountable for them. You choose the people, you will need to live by their decisions.

So, never rush in. You should always defer decisions that affect your people until you've involved them. If you're close to your people, it shouldn't take too long – a walk across the floor, a two-minute chat will produce a better decision than if you'd confined yourself to your office and made it yourself.

There are exceptions of course – a fire, a real crisis, or when you are in negotiation with a customer and have to make a decision there and then to get the business. In this latter case, you will have a mandate established beforehand. In other words, you will have asked other people before you come to a decision.

Never be frightened to ask people what they think. The more you ask, the more they will feel valued, the more they will feel that you respect them. It will enhance the contribution they make to the operation and, thus, enhance the effectiveness of the operation.

The paradox is that once you have established a high degree of mutual trust with your people, you won't need to ask them about certain types of decisions. They will trust you to make the right decisions and you will trust them too when they make decisions. Furthermore, they will trust that you will come and ask them if there is any uncertainty about a decision concerning them.

PRINCIPLE:
The best decisions are made when you ask the people affected by that decision.
People share responsibility for decisions they are involved in making.

PRACTICE:
Always pause before making a decision (unless it's a real crisis). Go through in your mind who you should be asking to ensure that an effective decision is made.

71

Be lenient

From time to time, you have to accept the unacceptable.

It is a truism to say that none of us is perfect. It's the reality. Regrettably, many bosses expect their people to be perfect, and spend much of their time castigating them for their imperfections.

The difficulty is the extent to which you should tolerate imperfections. Should you turn a blind eye to minor imperfections? Should you step in *every* time somebody infringes the standards you are so keen to maintain? Should you be meticulous in drawing people's attention to inadvertent errors?

The dilemma is great. If you turn a blind eye, you fear that your people will take advantage of you, will replicate these irritating imperfections. If you consistently pick up on them, then you fear that your people will see you as a busy-body, a pernickety perfectionist who is never satisfied, no matter how hard they try.

In my view, you must err on the side of your people. Tolerance and understanding of human failing is a key attribute for any boss. Never set out to punish or create a punitive climate of intimidation and fear. People work best when they are not afraid of a backlash from their boss should something go wrong. Leniency is far more acceptable than intolerance when judging a boss. Witch-hunts and 'find the culprit' investigations are still prevalent in many organizations in the aftermath of failure. Far better to learn the lesson than execute the transgressor.

BE LENIENT

if the following things happen occasionally.

- People are late

- People don't keep you informed when you think they should

- A person loses an important document

- Someone gives wrong information to a customer

- A person fails to take the initiative to fix a problem

- A person forgets something

- Someone breaks a rule

- Policy is ignored and people do their own thing

- People get their facts wrong

- People misquote others

- A person is late delivering a key report

- Someone totally screws up (causing loss of production, failure to deliver to a customer, or whatever)

- A person inadvertently offends you

- Someone makes a bad decision (in your view)

Don't be lenient if any of the above consistently happens.

There is a limit to leniency, however, and if a person *consistently* fails to meet the required standards, in such a way that the business is damaged as a result, then it must be the duty of the boss to step in and take remedial action.

That will be unnecessary when a group of people takes responsibility for their own actions and sets their own standards in pursuit of agreed organizational goals. There is no need to worry about whether or not you are being lenient or intolerant if your people can make that judgement for you. The buzz-phrase is 'peer group pressure'. It works. If people are allowed to get on and achieve what they believe (and you agree) is best for the business, then they will take immense pride in delivering first-class products and services. In this pursuit of excellence your people will become the arbiters of any transgressions, any deviations. They will assess the setbacks and the shortfalls and decide on remedial action.

Your role is to ensure that the standards have been set in the first place and that there is an accepted method for dealing with any deviations from them. If you set yourself up as a judge of other people's behaviour, you force yourself to make judgements that, potentially, can alienate people. Far better to set yourself up as a counsellor, enabling people to make their own judgements on what is acceptable or otherwise.

Leniency and tolerance are all about values. We value certain behaviours and need to be lenient towards those who seem not to value them in the same way. When working with a group of people, the key is to get maximum convergence of these values. Imposition can never work. Nowadays, you cannot force people to change behaviours that you find unacceptable. All you can do as a boss is facilitate a process, helping them examine their own values and behaviours in comparison with those you advocate and the business requires. In the interim, you have to be lenient.

Bite your tongue when you observe something you don't like at work. Think carefully before rushing in to criticize people for their aberrations. Forget about punishment – it is a last-resort device that you should employ rarely. And, if that exceptional case does arise and you have to punish someone, be lenient. Always give a person another chance. Never make the penalty so great that the suffering outweighs the opportunity to learn. Excessive penalties lead to alienation, while leniency leads to cooperation and improvement.

PRINCIPLE:
Accepting other peoples' imperfections and mistakes.

PRACTICE:
Resist punishing people.

Treat transgressions as learning opportunities.

Don't rush into making judgements.

Encourage your people to make their own judgements.

72

Be fair

Fairness is one of the key criteria by which your people will judge you.

In 1911, Frederick Winslow Taylor did the world of management a great disservice with his book *The Principles of Scientific Management* (Harper, 1911). He led us to believe that all work activity can be measured objectively and that there was no place for subjective judgement in assessing performance.

As a result, nowadays we have the pseudo-scientific practice of performance appraisal, in which we try to exercise objectivity in assessing an individual's contribution. Even worse, we sometimes attempt to link that assessment to pay.

All the evidence suggests that such a practice is blatantly unfair. At first sight, this is a paradox. You try to be objective when judging people and end up being accused of being unfair! There is no doubt that most forms of individual performance-related pay *are* unfair. Such schemes tend to be divisive, demotivational and rarely achieve what they seek to achieve – better performance.

Therein is the lie. To be effective as a boss, you have to make subjective judgements about people. Attempts to be solely objective will normally result in unfairness. The reason is simple. Any judgement about a person requires the application of both heart and mind. The heart is the source of subjectivity, the mind the source of objectivity. A boss with a big heart is likely to be fairer than a boss with no heart at all (if you see what I mean).

Inevitably there are dangers. Vested interests, personal attraction, and instinctive dislikes can sway the heart and adversely influence decision making. But, conversely, solely relying on objective

225

measurement and analysis discounts critical emotional factors that have a bearing on the decision.

Being fair, therefore, is an exercise of both heart and mind. We're back to the age-old virtue of balance. Extremes are dangerous and lead to bias. The heart should balance the mind, and vice versa. Such balance is more likely to lead to fairness than an over-reliance on intellect or on emotion.

Fairness is a big test for a boss. People instinctively know when a boss is being fair, when everyone is getting a bite at the cherry, when everyone has an opportunity to say their piece, when everyone gets a look in, when everyone takes an equitable share of what's going, when everyone is treated equally, when everyone competes on a level playing ground, when the same rules apply to everyone, when no favours are given.

Dip into any organization and talk at random to various employees. You will find that what bugs them most is unfairness (as they see it). For example, when they get looked over for promotion, when they get a smaller pay increase than they think is reasonable, when they are left out of certain activities, when other people seem to benefit from all the exciting opportunities, when an élite of people are 'in' with the boss and others 'out', when the performance appraisal rates them average although they believe they're exceptional, when the boss is unaware of how hard they work, when the boss continually finds fault, when the boss is too busy to see them.

Everywhere, people are preoccupied with their perceptions of fairness and unfairness. Frequently they talk of little else. They talk of the unreasonable demands placed on them, the unreasonable constraints they have to work under, the unreasonable statements made by the top brass, the unreasonable decisions that flow out of the ivory tower. They talk of incomprehensible personnel policies that prevent you sacking poor performers or hiring first-class people.

You can make as many objective decisions as you like, but your people's assessment of you will always be subjective. Unless you introduce subjective criteria into your decision making, your people will always judge you to be unfair.

Fairness is about a merging of perceptions, about the convergence of personal values, about the sharing of expressed beliefs, about the development of mutual respect, about the interpretation of what is important for all of us.

People will always push for those bosses they see as fair. They will respect such bosses.

Sometimes, fairness requires no more than a simple explanation, perhaps indicating the beliefs and reasons behind difficult decisions. Fairness is about creating understanding. You can make the best decision in the world, but, unless you communicate it effectively, there is a risk that it will be seen as unfair. It is not just *what* you decide and say, but *how* you communicate it as well.

We tend to see the same things differently. It's the half-empty versus half-full jug syndrome again. Being a great boss is about trying to get a group of people to see the same things the same way. Achieve that and you'll be judged to be a fair boss. Fail and they will judge you as being unfair. There is nothing wrong with different perceptions, but they have to be carefully explored with the aim of achieving some degree of convergence.

The biggest bone of contention often centres on how hard a person works, on what their real contribution is, on the extent of a person's capabilities and potential. Objective testing in this area is limited. To achieve fair results, it has to be supplemented with a degree of subjective judgement.

When difficult issues rise, get your people to advise you on what they see as being a fair solution. Never assume that they will be unfair.

PRINCIPLE:
Fairness.

PRACTICE:
Work closely with your people to agree on standards of fairness.
Don't be frightened to let your heart intercede and provide balance when making difficult judgements about people.

73

Practise what you preach

There's little need to preach. It will be all too evident from what you practise.

This book might be free from jargon, but I can guarantee that you are going to get some well-worn clichés to work on. A few now follow.

WELL-WORN CLICHÉS

- Fine words and no action
- Lip-service management
- Say one thing, do another
- Look both ways at the same time
- Running with the hares, hunting with the hounds
- Having the opinion of the last person you spoke to
- Blows with the wind
- The 'yes boss' syndrome (three bags full boss!)
- A stab in the back
- The rat race
- The prima donna syndrome
- Scoring brownie points
- Playing the game
- Working the system to your own advantage

- He (she) who shouts loudest achieves least
- A two-faced bxxxxxd
- All hot air
- All wind and no guts (a windbag)
- Sending out conflicting signals
- Treat a person like a dog and they'll behave like a dog
- Pay peanuts, get monkeys
- A man (woman) of action
- Practise what you preach
- Practise makes perfect
- Leadership by example
- Actions speak louder than words
- You are as good as your word
- Mean what you say, say what you mean
- The world is your oyster
- You could trust them with your life (or to the ends of the earth)
- Making it happen, getting it done

Great ideas come by the bucket-load. Most are spilled by the wayside by preachers who can't see where they're going and have never delivered. Putting new ideas into practice (and carrying the can for it) is a thousand times more difficult than inventing them in the first place.

It's best to go and get some practice under your belt before you start preaching. It's no good extolling the virtues of 'caring for staff' unless you are seen to do so, day in and day out. The business world now echoes with virtuous statements made by well-meaning managers who completely fail to convert these precious words into reality.

So, if you 'care for your customers' go and care for them, now! Talk about it later. Credibility comes from putting fine words into practice, not from fine words alone. Forget the 'mission statements' and glossy brochures, forget the ringing phrases that copywriters dream up – all you need to do is get out there and do something about it! Forget about 'empowering your people', just sit down, talk with them, and listen. Try to help them pursue all their exciting ideas for improving the business. In fact, just let them get on and do it!

Encourage them to talk to you straight, to tell you what they *really* think, and then, perhaps, they will welcome you being honest with them. Forget about performance appraisal – that's the form the preacher invented!

Smile down the telephone, make tea for your people, pick up litter, be the first to take a pay cut when times are tough, sit on reception, delegate your own budget to the front line, let your people make your decisions, tear up the organization chart, get rid of all privileges, stay at home while your people travel abroad for you, be the first to attend the customer service training session, then attend every other session, bring in cakes, pursue at least one crazy idea every week, get your people to come up with crazy ideas, send postcards to your people when you're away on business, keep your people up to date, buy lunch for your people and watch a Tom Peter's video together, water the office flowers, invite your customers to the office party, abolish memos, ban ties, give a prize for the best suggestion for giving prizes, change the office lighting (add colour), use the small Day-Glo orange Post-it notes, never use surnames, buy a laptop computer for everyone, make keyboard skills mandatory, stop spending money – get your people to do it for you. *Practise what you preach.*

What do you preach? Track back through the last paragraph and try to discover the underlying principles. What is being preached by each of the stated practices? How do they align with your approach?

Preaching is all right, providing you remember the following:

- don't do it very often

- when you do, make sure it's based on your *own* beliefs, not on anyone else's

- the beliefs you preach can be demonstrated by your own personal practice.

PRINCIPLE:
You must have principles, but you don't need to go around preaching them.

PRACTICE:
Whatever you practise must be based on your own principles, not those of others.

Whatever your principles are, you must practise them.

74

Make yourself available

The boss is a resource that people should always find available.

Some people are quite capable of working by themselves for weeks, if not months, on end. They deliver the results required of them without needing to frequently refer to their boss. They self-start, fix problems, and generally take liberties to achieve great success.

These people, though, are rare. Most people demand time with their boss. They will require direction, clarification, support, feedback, and praise.

And herein lies a dilemma for a great boss. By being too available, by giving too much time, people begin to rely on their boss for everything. They turn to them for the simplest of decisions, they fail to take initiatives, preferring those of the boss. They become dependent on having a boss around. The boss becomes their crutch.

Conversely, prolonged and frequent absence by the boss poses dangers of lack of control, of things getting out of hand, of decisions not being made, and solutions to urgent problems being delayed.

Common sense dictates no one answer to this dilemma. A boss should be available, but *how* available will depend on the circumstances of the people themselves. Certain individuals will need more time than others. The complexity of the problem, the nature of the task, the pressures being applied, as well as the capability of the individual, are all variables that have to be judged when assessing the appropriate level of availability.

As often, it is a question of balance. To strike it right requires sensitive antennae and a highly developed understanding between yourself (as boss) and your people.

RICHARD BRANSON

'Richard Branson ensures that every employee at Virgin Atlantic has his home telephone number and they are encouraged to ring him any time should there be a need'.

Availability is not the same as presence. Availability is like being a port of call, except you don't have to call. Availability is about being there when needed. There is no universal prescription for such need, but only intuition (gained through understanding) will tell you when it is most likely to arise.

Availability is about priorities. It means putting your people first so that when they call on you, you drop everything for them, but it is also about helping them learn that they have no need to call on you too often, that they are able to deal with situations that they might have referred to you before.

Availability is giving your people peace of mind, allowing them to rest assured that you can be reached in times of crisis or when urgent support is required.

It is also about initiating frequent contact with them and, therefore, minimizing reactive demands on your time. Make sure you see your people on a regular basis so that they can control their demands on your time. If they know you walk around at 8.30 a.m. every morning or meet with them at 3.00 p.m. every Friday afternoon, the probability is that they will keep routine items for then and only demand additional time if something out of the ordinary arises. Providing a framework of regular sessions with you creates availability. Without such a framework, you and your people drift into uncontrollable reactive mode.

24-HOUR AVAILABILITY

'One of the best bosses I ever had always used to walk around first thing in the morning and ask how things were going. He might only spend a minute with each of us, but it was a golden opportunity to raise issues that had arisen the previous day and to update each other on various matters.

Furthermore, he would have a regular monthly one-hour slot with us individually to talk through ongoing items.

Finally, he would go out of his way to make himself available if we wanted to see him at other times. Normally he'd find time for us within 24 hours. I would ring up and say "Mike, can I pop in to see you?", and he'd reply, "I'm tied up till 5.30 p.m. but I'd be happy to see you then". No matter how busy he was, he always made himself available.'

In summary, there is no set answer as to how often you should see your people. The decision should really be theirs. The key is to give top priority to finding a slot for your people should they want to see you. If they do place excessive demands on your time, simply talk it through with them, develop a closer understanding. You will need to help them stand on their own two feet rather than place too much reliance on you.

PRINCIPLE:
Making yourself available to your people when they have need of you.

PRACTICE:
Create a schedule of regular sessions with your people, individually and in groups, so that they can have access to you.

Encourage your people not to be excessively reliant on you.

Assign the highest priority to seeing your people when they ask for you.

75

Know where to draw the line

The line is the agreed standard.

One of the boss' jobs is to draw the line between what is acceptable and what is not acceptable at work. The issue of unacceptable behaviour has already been dealt with in a previous section, but equally important is the issue of substandard work.

This can be a difficult area. I know bosses who insist on seeing every letter sent out of the section and who frequently rewrite those letters, ensuring that the grammar is correct, the punctuation is in order, and that nothing contentious or confusing is said. There are other bosses who are such perfectionists that nothing ever gets done.

Imperfection has to be tolerated, but to what degree?

Most people know what is totally unacceptable as well as thoroughly acceptable, but in between is a confusing area of standards that are acceptable to some but not others. Handwritten reports might be acceptable in one organization, but not in another. Some people prefer their reception areas to have a 'lived in' feel to them while others like to have a reception that is exceptionally clean and tidy, with not a single magazine out of place on a gleaming, dust-free glass coffee table.

What is certain is that customers will expect increasingly high standards of services and products from their suppliers. It will not be acceptable for a service engineer to turn up later than the specified time, or for there to be a shortage on the order, or for calls not to be returned. Frequent failures will result in loss of business.

To achieve the high standards required, a boss has to ensure that the line is drawn very clearly for all to see. Furthermore, they have to ensure that the line is seen to be fair and reasonable by the people who will have to maintain it.

The line doesn't only apply to big issues, such as punctual deliveries, but also to issues of detail. Many bosses shy away from the latter, fearful of being seen as nit-pickers or faultfinders, but to the customer, it is often the detail that creates a bad impression, which can go against a company. It is the greasy fingermarks on the side of the brand new photocopier just delivered. It is spelling a customer's name incorrectly or using a wrong title. It is sending out an invoice for work already paid for. Sometimes it is simply forgetting to do something.

As soon as the line has been agreed, it is up to the boss and their people to ensure that it is kept to. There is no point in having a line unless there is some monitoring and feedback process to

---

THE LINE

(examples)

- **99.9 per cent punctuality**
- **All calls returned within eight hours**
- **All letters replied to within two days**
- **One spelling mistake per 100 letters**
- **Customers' names and addresses always correct**
- **All promises kept**
- **Immaculate appearance (anything delivered to a customer to be spotless)**
- **Figures always add up and always double-checked**
- **With rare exceptions, all letters to be written in a warm and friendly manner, to make the recipient feel good (very few cold, formal, factual letters)**
- **Clear desks every evening (no papers left lying around)**
- **Incredibly hospitable reception**

---

show this. To maintain standards, you must have measures, no matter how detailed the standards.

As a boss, you will need to take action when the line is infringed. You will need to examine the reasons, to establish whether or not there has been some misunderstanding, some genuine mistake or mere complacency on the part of one of your people. If you turn a blind eye to people consistently stepping over the line, then others will notice and there will be a rapid deterioration of standards within your unit. You might tolerate the occasional transgression, but not on repeated occasions.

To monitor standards, you do not need an elaborate, bureaucratic system. Common sense is best applied in determining whether or not the line is being kept to. Random sampling through regular observation is often adequate. You don't even need to keep a record in most cases.

When you come across an instance of substandard work always ask for an explanation first, before you jump to conclusions. Then agree a way of rectifying the situation to ensure that the line is kept to from then on. Don't go round blaming people and punishing them for substandard work. What you need to do is help them to come up to standard.

PRINCIPLE:
Maintenance of the highest possible standards.

PRACTICE:
Work with your people to ensure that the standards are clearly defined.

Develop a common-sense method of monitoring the levels attained in relation to each standard.

Always give constructive and helpful feedback and advice in order to make improvements.

76

Mean what you say and say what you mean

People crave sincerity in their bosses.

Here's another cliché: 'You cannot pull the wool over people's eyes all the time'. Here are some related rules: never 'snow' people with too much data, never be economical with the truth, never say one thing and do another. Attempt any of these cons (manipulations) and you will be doomed to the pits of distrust and disrespect. Your credibility will diminish. Your people will not 'rate' you.

People want bosses who are straight with them, who do not play games, who do not manipulate, who do not run with the hares and hunt with the hounds, who do not compete in the 'rat race', who do not exploit situations for brownie points.

People want bosses who say what they mean and mean what they say. The old-fashioned word for this is 'integrity'. If you demonstrate a lack of integrity, your people will go against you, they will play you at your own game. You will not get at the facts, the truth will be hidden.

To say what you mean and mean what you say, you have to know yourself. You have to have belief in as well as the courage of your convictions. If you lack these you will appease people by saying what they want to hear, you will fudge over problems, you will make false promises, you will hedge your bets. You will not commit but defer instead.

If you declare an intention always carry it out. So, if you *say* you are going to review someone's salary in six months' time, *review* it in six months' time – irrespective of pressures from others not to do so. If you promise training make sure it is provided. If you say there will be a decision next week make sure that there *is* a decision next week. If you declare in a speech that people are your business' most important asset you must demonstrate what you mean with good, consistent practice, otherwise your words are meaningless. Similarly, if you exhort your people to put the customer first, then every opportunity must be seized to do so, by you as well as them.

So many senior executives say one thing and do another. Frequently there is little correlation between the bland generalizations about company intent (for example, in annual reports) and the reality of what people experience first hand. To quote: 'We listen to our customers, we listen to our staff', but where's the evidence? The customers don't feel listened to and the staff certainly don't. Also, 'We welcome your views and are happy to receive suggestions', but what is done with these views and suggestions? In many cases, nothing. Then there's: 'We strive to achieve the highest quality and provide the highest standards of service', but when the product is faulty, customers can't get through on the phone. Another is: 'We pride ourselves on our communications with our employees', but, more often than not, your employees find out things by watching the local news on television or reading the local newspapers. These phrases become 'hot air', 'fine words and no action'.

So, here is the challenge. Never use words loosely. Always ensure that you can support everything you say. Always be serious when you make a declaration of intent. If you say 'We must get together for lunch soon', you must *mean* it. If you say 'I think you're doing a great job', you must mean it. Never appease. Appeasement misleads.

There are bosses who can charm you off your feet one minute, then give you hell the next, who can make you feel like royalty one day, but the lowest of the low the next. You might adapt, you might even like it. After all, it gives you something to talk about. In all probability, though, you will hate it.

So, what do you want to be like as a boss? What sort of reputation do you want? Do you want to be straight or crooked? Do you want to be trusted or do you want to play the game? Alan Clarke is very eloquent about the game of politics: 'If you are a serious player, it's no good being "straight". You just won't last!' (*Diaries*, Weidenfeld & Nicolson, 1993). Do you want to be like a politician?

I know what my personal preference is. I like people I can trust, who are straight. Furthermore I really do believe that people work effectively together and perform to high standards when there is a high degree of trust, when they know where they stand with each other.

It's all to do with sincerity, integrity, credibility, and mutual respect, as well as trust. There is no easy route to acquiring these qualities other than to continually challenge yourself.

Saying what you mean, and meaning what you say is something you have to apply to every single statement you make at work. You have to be consistent in its practice. Every activity you undertake, every behaviour has to be consistent with these statements. You've really got to strive hard not to mislead, to make sure that there can be no possible misinterpretation of what you say. It's hard work, but it will reflect the strengths of your beliefs.

PRINCIPLE:
Integrity and sincerity.

PRACTICE:
Thinking before you speak.

Knowing that whatever you *say* you are going to do you will *actually* do.

Taking care to communicate clearly about your actions to minimize any risk of misinterpretation.

77

Defer to your people

Show your respect for your people by deferring to them.

In the traditional hierarchical organization difficult decisions are always referred to the boss. It is assumed, incorrectly at times, that because people are bosses they have accumulated sufficient wisdom, knowledge, skills and experience to handle *any* decisions put to them.

So decisions are bounced upwards. Traditional bosses like this because it makes them feel important and it gives them power. Their people like it, too, because it absolves them from the responsibility of making difficult decisions. So, if something goes wrong it is easy to blame the boss.

In practice, bosses are *not* always in the best position to make difficult decisions. To do so they have to rely on information and advice provided by their people, in which case it is more sensible to have their people make the decision, and make them accountable for it.

The way decisions are handled distinguishes a great boss from a poor one. The latter will attempt to soak up as many decisions as possible to enhance their power and status. However, the great boss, forever humble, respects the fact that his (or her) people know more, have better information, are closer to the situation, and, therefore, frequently defers to their better judgement.

However, in deferring to your people, clear boundaries have to be drawn, outside of which they cannot make decisions. For example, they should only be allowed to make any decisions having a direct impact on their own area of responsibility, not ones that have a consequential impact on other sections or departments. For example, your people should be able to make decisions on how best to organize their own work, on what training they should have within agreed budgets, on when to order fresh supplies for their section. What they *cannot* do is make decisions about such things as changing company procedures or commandeering equipment or office space. Inevitably, these boundaries should be based on common sense. You have to trust your people not to do anything outrageous, like take everyone off the section at the same time (for training) without providing cover.

Deferring to your people becomes an essential discipline of management. It is all too easy to fall into the trap of making decisions *for* your people. It can be flattering when they come and ask 'We have a problem here boss, what should we do?' Too many bosses succumb to the temptation of providing a quick fix to their people's problems.

Deferring to your people does make it tough for them: they have to make and be accountable for the decisions affecting their work.

There is a thin line between offering advice and appearing to make a decision. If you see your role (as you should) as providing support to your people, then it is quite proper, when your people are in a fix, to offer suggestions and propose solutions. However, it is up to them whether or not to take up your suggestions. If your advice is too forceful, too adamant, the decision will appear to be yours and you will effectively remove accountability from them. So, don't encourage your people to bring their problems to you, otherwise you will burden yourself with a plethora of advice giving and apparent decision making and you will flip back to being an old-fashioned autocratic boss who holds all the reins and is bogged down in trivia. What you must do is refuse to make decisions when your people bring problems to you! Only they can decide, especially if the decision is within their own boundary.

The parallels with family life are useful here. You cannot *tell* people who to marry, or whether or not to have children, or whether or not to separate when things get rough, or to divorce. These are *their* decisions, not anyone else's. At best, others offer advice.

Regrettably, too many bosses take on decisions that are not theirs, but should be those of their people. The only time the boss should make decisions affecting their people is when they cannot agree on the right approach among themselves.

THE UNACCEPTABLE BOSS

'The trouble with our boss is that he never accepts what we say. He goes through the motions of listening to us, but he never takes on board anything we tell him. It's like he's humouring us all the time. It seems he thinks he always knows best, that our ideas won't work, are not practical. If we push him a little harder to pursue something, he gets defensive, as if we are getting at him for not having thought of the idea in the first place. He seems to have an answer for everything. It's very frustrating. Most of us have given up now - you can never make any headway with him.'

PRINCIPLE:
The person who knows best should make the decisions.

The boss doesn't always know best.

PRACTICE:
Offer advice, yes, but refuse to make decisions when your people call for them. Get them to make the decisions (providing this doesn't impact other sections/departments).

78

Challenge yourself

Today everything about your job and your work is being challenged. It's best you challenge yourself first rather than react and lose out to the challenge presented by others.

Challenge is a driving force in life and at work. If you avoid challenge you will be left behind as your competitors move ahead.

Your organization might well set the challenges for you, but, as a great boss, you will want to set your *own* challenges – the challenges of improving quality, customer service, motivation. The challenge of innovation, of being creative. The challenge of cutting down on waste, of improving systems. The challenge of improving the working environment, of making your people's jobs more enjoyable. The challenge of outclassing the competition – internally when it comes to promotion, externally when other companies bid for your business.

In days of old, the status quo might have been a viable option. Things rarely changed, customers were loyal, employees were loyal, tried and trusted procedures never varied, everyone did what they were told to do, and virtually did the same thing every day for years on end.

Now everything has changed. Nothing is certain. There is no security of employment, not even in public service. Competition is seeping into every facet of our lives. Nothing comes on a plate any longer. Whether we like it or not we are being forced to pay directly for more and more things that previously we had taken for granted came for free – like health care, entrance to museums, higher education. And like the internal services provided by central departments at work.

We can no longer rest on our laurels and avoid competition by working for large, secure organizations, guaranteeing employment through to retirement because they no longer exist.

The challenge each one of us has today is that we have to justify our own existence continually to survive. If we cannot prove we are adding value to the organization, then the likelihood is that we will be fired. It is no good waiting for the organization to tell us that we are valued (just because they hired us in the first place), the onus is on us to demonstrate it. Senior executives change, competition becomes fiercer, new technology comes in, and, suddenly, the values change. The contribution you were making five years ago might well have been highly valued then, but today it might have no value at all.

As a boss in today's world, you will continually have to prove yourself. That's the challenge. You will need to find better ways of doing things, of being innovative, constantly increasing your standards. A delivery reliability of 95 per cent on the specified day might have been acceptable in the past, but tomorrow customers will want a delivery reliability of 99.95 per cent within a specified 2-hour 'window'. You have to be ahead of the competition all the time in pushing up the standards of what can be delivered in the future. This applies to internal services as much as to external services.

Setting challenges, therefore, becomes a vital task for any boss. Protecting the status quo cannot be an option, the competition will not allow it even if your organization does.

Many people shudder at the prospect of fiercer competition, fearing for their jobs. It is a negative view. It is seeing life as a threat. However, the process of working with your people to set even tougher challenges, and then meeting them, can prove exception-ally exhilarating. Everything *is* possible! If the competition can do it, why can't you? Why should the competition be any better than you?

First and foremost, in setting challenges you have to challenge yourself. You have to think through carefully what you are there for as a boss, what you are really seeking to achieve. It cannot be a life of comfort and security, relatively free of pain. You have no option but to push yourself and your people to the limits of what you are capable of achieving. Amazingly, in doing so you will discover that you are capable of achieving much more than you ever thought you would in the first place. By setting tough challenges, people invariably surprise themselves by meeting them!

EXAMPLES OF BRITISH COMPANIES THAT HAVE RISEN TO THE CHALLENGE

Oxford Automotive Components*	Guinness*
United Distillers*	Tube Investments (TI Group)*
The Virgin Group*	ICL*
Control Techniques*	British Gas
British Airways	The Body Shop
Waterstones	

* All case studies in an excellent book *The British Renaissance*, by Jeffrey Ferry (Heinemann, 1993).

Sit down with your people and challenge them: 'What could we really do over the next few months or years that could outclass the competition?' If you can identify this and pursue it, you will really learn a lot about yourself and your people. You will learn how great you all are! Most people have greatness lurking within them, but it takes a great boss to exploit it. That's the challenge!

PRINCIPLE:
In business, the vital driving force is the challenge of increasing competition.

PRACTICE:
Work closely with your people to clearly identify the challenges, keep them in mind and drive towards meeting them.

79

Never give up

Keep moving towards what you want to achieve and don't stop until you get there.

Never give up. There are more defeatists in life than winners. If life was that easy, we would all be incredibly successful, incredibly rich, and there would be no problems. Life is difficult for most of us. It's full of pitfalls, obstacles and setbacks intended to deter us. Those who make progress push aside these barriers and keep moving forward.

Work is no different. It is *meant* to be difficult – competition ensures that. In fact progress is a *function* of difficulty and competition. Without it there would be rapid decay and things would be even worse. Consequently, no manager can ever have an easy ride. Every day will bring an avalanche of problems, external and internal. Your competitors will change the ground rules, they will lower prices just as you are putting yours up, they will bring out a new product that is far superior to yours (if you dare admit it), they will persuade one of your major customers to ditch you and switch to them. Your factory will be smitten with operating problems, machines will develop intermittent faults that cannot be traced, you will lose vital production through excessive down-time, your warehouse will be broken into, your computer operator will go down with flu. And those are just the easy problems on the nursery slopes of the mountain you are climbing. But, they *can* be solved.

The difficult problems invariably revolve around the people you work with – people who don't seem cooperative, who never communicate, who try to stab you in the back, who claim the glory for *your* achievements, who are totally cynical and negative. These are the problems that you are paid to crack as a boss.

However, your greatest problem will be your greatest challenge, and that is how to keep moving forward on what you really want to achieve. Successful people have an exceptionally clear vision of their future success and it is this that drives them forwards. It might be a vision of winning a gold medal in the Olympics, or developing your own highly successful business. Most people set their sights a little lower, but that doesn't mean to say that they shouldn't have sights.

As soon as you are clearly focused on what you want to achieve, you must persist in making progress, irrespective of problems, taking setbacks in your stride, overcoming obstacles, tackling people who try to throw you off course.

If you want to learn more about never giving up, study the lives of successful people. Read the stories of Anita Roddick (*Body and Soul*, Ebury Press, 1991), Richard Branson (Mick Brown, *The Inside Story*, Michael Joseph, 1988), and a few others. Look at Linford Christie, Tina Turner, and some of the other sports and pop stars of today. How did *they* make it?

Ultimately it is a deep-rooted belief in themselves that drives these people on. If they can make it, why not you? What's so special about

---

QUALITIES OF THOSE WHO NEVER GIVE UP

- Tenacity
- Perseverance
- Determination
- Resolve
- Steadfastness
- Single-mindedness
- Relentlessness
- Guts
- Stamina
- Persistence
- High degree of self-belief

- Resilience
- Courage
- Firmness
- Fortitude
- Courage
- Indefatigability
- Strong backbone
- Grit
- Inexorability
- Vision

248

successful people? Nothing, except that they never give up, they drive themselves on and on towards success. They are never defeated, they never allow the world to convince them that they are ordinary, that they don't have the qualitites of the superstars, that they cannot achieve outstanding results.

Look at the work you are doing, look at your responsibilities, look at what the organization expects of you, at what your people expect of you. Then reflect on all this and set your sights high. Get your people and your boss to provide the essential support for climbing that high mountain. They will want you to succeed as much as you do. It will be their success too. When you feel like giving up they will urge you on. The reverse also applies.

There will be times when you have been knocked down and you think you will never get there, but don't quit! Try again. If you don't succeed first time, try a second time and then a third, and, if necessary, a thousand times. From all the success stories there is enough evidence to indicate that if you keep on trying, the probability of being successful increases. If you *believe* you can, you *will* get there in the end. As soon as you stop believing you can do it, you will fail.

Examine the qualities listed above. There is no earthly reason why you should not demonstrate most of them. What is life all about but achieving a measure of success at work, home, and play? Never give up in your pursuit of this success.

PRINCIPLE:
To be successful, you have to keep on trying.

PRACTICE:
Eliminate any thoughts that you are not as good as other people in your chosen pursuit (at work or elsewhere).

Keep looking for better ways of doing things. Learn from your mistakes. Never give up in trying to achieve what you want to achieve.

80

One more thing: you must deliver!

The ultimate test for a great boss is what he (or she) delivers.

You *have* to deliver something, otherwise you shouldn't be there. As a great boss you will need to have an exceptionally clear picture in your mind of what this is.

All the other points made in this book become irrelevant unless they are geared towards producing an excellent bottom-line result. That's what you are paid for and that's what you must deliver.

For it to be delivered, it must be measured and that's where many organizations fall down. Managers are left with vague job descriptions and ill-defined objectives without any effective measure of the service or product they have to deliver. So nobody knows how well they're doing. Often they don't even know if they're doing the right thing. Therefore, the end result must be kept in sharp focus. There is no point in hiring the best people, training them, praising and encouraging them if it is not all directed towards achievements valued by your organization (as well as yourself).

However focusing on the result to be delivered is not as simple as that. Too often there is the criticism of 'short termism'. It has been said again and again, but it is valid enough to assert again here, short-term goals are often achieved at the expense of the long-term ones. A great boss needs to be clear about *both* types. Neither should be achieved at the expense of the other. To achieve credibility, a great boss will deliver both in the short term and the long term.

An excellent discipline is to carry out a periodic review of what you are paid to deliver, initially by listing your main bottom-line objectives. It shouldn't take too long. In fact, a long list will probably mean that your objectives are out of focus and that your efforts are being diluted. Having reviewed your list, sit down and discuss it with your boss. Is it in accord with what he or she thinks? Then, involve your people and make sure they are perfectly clear about what has to be achieved and what their part in all this is.

It is no good coming up with objectives like 'We are going to deliver the best customer service in the region'. Far better to be specific and state your intention to, say, deliver telephone responses in which 98 per cent of calls are answered within five seconds, to reduce the lead time from date of order to date of receipt from two weeks to two days, to demonstrate (by use of a survey) that your people have a friendlier and more helpful approach to your customers than any of your competitors.

You might aim to deliver the very best quality, but that, too, has to be defined. The best-quality coffee served to visitors? The best-quality toilets? The best-quality reception service? The best-quality car-parking arrangements? The most reliable and fault-free products?

The processes of definition and measurement are critical when identifying what you have to deliver. Furthermore, what you have to deliver has to be challenging. If it's routine and has been readily done for the last ten years, then you can hardly claim credit for delivering it because you may as well not have been there. A great boss secures challenging delivery objectives.

Other delivery objectives might relate to change – for example, streamlining an organization to drive out central costs, or exploiting the vast reservoir of talent you have to generate increased revenue. They might relate to developing new markets and increasing market share or introducing exciting new products. They could relate to developing a valuable new central service required by line managers.

Therefore, the last question in this book, and, perhaps, the most important one, is 'What are you there to deliver?' If you don't know, you can never be a great boss. You must determine this if you don't know. Once you have that essential direction, then you can put into play all the other things mentioned in this book.

Finally, you have to believe you *can* deliver. After all, if *you* don't do it, someone else *will*. That's the way the world works nowadays. It's called competition and it extends everywhere. The great bosses are those who deliver ahead of the competition. That's your challenge. There is nothing magical about meeting the challenge, it's all about putting some common-sense principles into practice. Most of them are listed in the eighty sections of this book. Put them into practice, be clear about what you have to deliver, deliver it and you really will be a great boss!

PRINCIPLE:
The importance of delivering a clear, measurable result.

PRACTICE:
List what you have to deliver, both in the short term and long term.

Ensure that there are clear, tangible measures for each delivery objective.

Ensure that your own boss and your people endorse and support these delivery objectives.

Put into practice the common-sense principles expounded in previous sections of this book, then go and deliver!